DRAGONS ENTANGLED

Indochina and the China–Vietnam War

Steven J. Hood

DRAGONS ENTANGLED

DRAGONS ENTANGLED

Indochina and the China–Vietnam War

Steven J. Hood

An East Gate Book

M. E. Sharpe Inc.
Armonk, New York
London, England

An East Gate Book

Library of Congress Cataloging-in-Publication Data

Hood, Steven J.
Dragons entangled: Indo-China and the China-Vietnam War /
by Steven J. Hood.
p.   cm.
Includes bibliographical references and index.
ISBN 0-87332-862-0 (c); ISBN 1-56324-270-2 (p)
1. Sino-Vietnamese Conflict, 1979.
2. Indochina—History—1945–
I. Title
DS559.916.H66   1992
959.704′4—dc20
91-10743
CIP

Printed in the United States of America

The paper used in this publication meets the minimum requirements of
American National Standard for Information Sciences—
Permanence of Paper for Printed Library Materials,
ANSI Z39.48–1984.

MV (c)   10   9   8   7   6   5   4   3   2
MV (p)   10   9   8   7   6   5   4   3   2   1

To my parents, John and Joyce Hood,
and my grandfather, LeCoy Anderson

Contents

List of Tables and Maps

Tables

Maps

Acknowledgments

I am indebted to Professor Alan P. L. Liu of the University of California, Santa Barbara, for his guidance and criticisms of this work. Professors Wolfram Hanrieder and Michael Gordon, also at Santa Barbara, helped with the basic theoretical framework of the study. I am also grateful to my colleagues Nicholas Berry, Gerard Fitzpatrick, and Paul Stern for their encouragement and support.

Portions of Chapter 4 appeared in "Beijing's Cambodian Gamble and Prospects for Peace in Indochina: The Khmer Rouge or Sihanouk?" by Steven J. Hood. *Asian Survey,* vol. 30, no. 10, October 1990, pp. 977–91. Copyright © 1990 by the Regents of the University of California, used with permission.

An anonymous reader on behalf of M. E. Sharpe suggested some format changes that clarified the organization of the book. I greatly appreciate these suggestions.

Special acknowledgment goes to my wife Mary, for her copyediting and help with the maps. In a deeper sense, her interest and encouragement in my work has always been my primary reward for hard work.

Abbreviations

ASEAN	Association of Southeast Asian Nations
CCP	Chinese Communist Party
CGDK	Coalition Government of Democratic Kampuchea
COMECON	(or CMEA), Council for Mutual Economic Assistance
DK	Democratic Kampuchea
DRV	Democratic Republic of Vietnam
FBIS	Foreign Broadcast Information Service
FEER	Far Eastern Economic Review
GMD	Guomindang
ICP	Indochina Communist Party
JIM	Jakarta Informal Meeting
JPRS	Joint Publications Research Service
KCP	Kampuchean Communist Party
KNUFNS	Kampuchean National United Front for National Salvation
KPNLF	Kampuchean Peoples National Liberation Front
KR	Khmer Rouge
NCNA	New China News Agency
NVA	North Vietnamese Army
PLA	People's Liberation Army
PRC	People's Republic of China
PRG	Provisional Revolutionary Government
PRK	People's Republic of Kampuchea
ROC	Republic of China

ROV   Republic of Vietnam
SNC   Supreme National Council
SRV   Socialist Republic of Vietnam
USSR   Union of Soviet Socialist Republics
VCP   Vietnamese Communist Party

Introduction

Dragons Entangled:
A Marathon Conflict

On February 14, 1979, the People's Liberation Army (PLA) of the People's Republic of China (PRC) launched a full-scale military assault across the southern border of China into the Socialist Republic of Vietnam (SRV). The invasion followed months of tense relations between the two nations, though the sudden action surprised many who doubted China's resolve actually to attack its neighbor. The war between the two Asian Communist countries, like the conflict between China and the Soviet Union, accentuates deep tensions between supposedly "fraternal" nations with socialist ideologies.

Very few people inside and outside the interdisciplinary realm of East Asian studies understand the importance of this war. Millions of people have been affected by it, both in Vietnam, along the Sino-Vietnamese border, and in Cambodia and Laos where Hanoi and Beijing have carried out much of their struggles. Official estimates put the number of people killed as a result of this conflict since 1978 to be well over 500,000.[1] Yet despite an occasional glance at the conflict by the Western press, very little attention has been paid to this serious rift that sours the prospects for peace not only in Southeast Asia, but threatens the whole East Asian region as well.

There are several reasons for the lack of attention given to the this conflict, among them:

1. The West, particularly the United States, has lost interest in the region, in part because of the cost of involvement in Vietnam during the past several decades;

2. Scholarship on Asian topics has focused primarily on what are perceived to be the "major issues" of East Asia—Japan-U.S. trade rifts, China's domestic reforms and opening to the outside world, and the emergence of the newly industrializing countries of South Korea, Taiwan, Hong Kong, and Singapore;

3. Most importantly, a lack of appreciation of the seriousness that this conflict poses not only for China and Vietnam, but for the stability of Southeast Asia and extending into East Asia generally.

With these points in mind, this book attempts to bring to light the causes and dynamics of the Sino-Vietnamese conflict. It has been written in a manner that can be easily understood by the informed nonspecialist, and yet enlighten the Asian scholar or specialist in conflict studies seeking a greater understanding of this ongoing power struggle. It is mostly a political/historical work that takes into consideration many of the regional, cultural, and economic factors that figure prominently in the China-Vietnam relationship.

From this interdisciplinary approach, one factor plays more importance in understanding this conflict than any other. The most important point of conflict between China and Vietnam is a common desire to be the dominant power in Indochina. But this factor cannot be looked at independently because it has been complicated by a number of other factors. Strategically, due to Vietnam's own long-range concerns, the Soviet Union has been involved in the power struggle in order to give Hanoi added clout in opposing China. Washington, too, has been a factor in the conflict, though American policy makers have not been as interested in a settlement as they should have been. Finally, as the competition for Indochina heated up between Hanoi and Beijing, so did the importance of several irritants, namely, the territorial border dispute between the two nations, and the presence of ethnic Chinese living in Vietnam.

This work, then, seeks to present a comprehensive interpretation of the Sino-Vietnamese conflict. It covers not only the strategic and regional concerns of Beijing and Hanoi, but the role of the superpowers, and the importance of irritants in the dispute— points often overlooked when considering the China-Vietnam conflict.

A wide variety of sources have been consulted in preparing this book. Whenever possible, primary resource material from the Socialist Republic of Vietnam, the various Cambodian factions, and the People's Republic of China have been used to support my main arguments. This has not always been easy, as obtaining information from the Vietnamese and Cambodians is difficult. Most documents of significance have been translated in the Foreign Broadcast Information Service (FBIS) *Daily Report*, and the U.S. Commerce Department Joint Publication Research Service (JPRS) series. Various United Nations documents have also been referred to which contain official statements on the conflict.

Government documents from the Chinese side are more readily available. Beijing has published several small books on Sino-Vietnamese relations which provide insight into many aspects of the conflict. Many of these sources have been reprinted in the *Beijing Review* and other publications, as well as in the FBIS and JPRS translations.

Other primary resource materials have been gathered from the UC Berkeley Indochina Archives collection. These include various documents released by the Hanoi authorities, and declassified and unclassified U.S. documents that deal with the subject at hand. Major dailies from Asia, the United States, and other Western countries have also been consulted. Some secondary materials have proven useful, especially in chapter one which deals with the historical relationship between China and Vietnam.

The first chapter of this work reviews the historical relationship between China and Vietnam, when some seeds of mutual distrust were sown. The next three chapters then consider China and Vietnam's immediate differences over the balance of power in Indochina. These include attention to the superpowers, the United Nations, the role of the ASEAN nations, and the various Cambodian factions—all of which have tried to get an upper hand in the conflict from different vantage points. Chapter five is devoted to an explanation of the problems of borders and territories under dispute and chapter six to the conflict surrounding ethnic Chinese living in Vietnam. A summary and conclusion follows.

DRAGONS
ENTANGLED

1

Historical Background: Chinese and Vietnamese Relations to 1975

Henceforth our country is safe.
Our mountains and rivers begin life afresh.
Peace follows war as day follows night.
We have purged our shame for a thousand centuries.
We have regained tranquility for ten-thousand generations.

—Vietnamese poem celebrating the turning back
of a full-scale Chinese attack in 1788

It is easy to overestimate or underestimate the role of history when considering causes leading to conflicts between nation-states. Such is the case with Vietnam and China. There is a tendency by some scholars to point to longstanding rifts between China and Vietnam to prove that recent disagreements are but a reflection of historic differences. Others argue the historical picture has little to offer those looking for causes of recent problems between the two nations.

Regardless of what outside observers say about the historical importance of China and Vietnam's relationship, it is important at this point to consider what each side has to say about its shared past. In calling for peace talks and continued negotiations with Vietnam, Beijing refers to the "historic friendship" that

3

has existed between the two countries, adding that recent problems can be corrected.[1] Hanoi's white paper of 1979 indicates the present problems have grown in recent decades:

> The Chinese leaders' acts of open hostility against Vietnam, culminating in their war of aggression started on February 17, 1979, have astonished world public opinion by the sudden shift of China's policy toward Vietnam. Yet, this policy shift was to be expected. It was, in fact, a logical development of the expansionist and hegemonistic strategy pursued by the Chinese leaders over the past three decades. . . .
>
> U.S. imperialism, formerly considered as the most dangerous enemy "whose character would never change," is now regarded as a reliable ally, and the Chinese who are colluding with it have brazenly declared that China is an "Eastern NATO."[2]

It would appear from these examples that the root of the conflict may indeed be a result of recent strains and not necessarily the product of centuries of conflict. But to overlook the long history of relations between the two countries would be a mistake for several reasons. First, Vietnam owes much of its tradition and current outlook toward other nation-states to its historic domination by its larger neighbor to the north. Second, and directly related to the first reason, Vietnam has had relations with China far longer than with any other nation. In fact, China and Vietnam have had relations with each other longer than most nations have been around. Finally, looking into the historic past of these two countries leads to greater insight in seeking to understand current Chinese-Vietnamese relations.

This chapter consists of three sections. The first section will cover the history of Vietnamese and Chinese relations from Vietnam's beginnings to the tenth century A.D. The second section looks at their relationship to the period of French colonization of Vietnam. The third section considers Vietnam's struggle for independence from France and its growing rift with China to about 1975. A short summary will follow.

The Birth of Vietnam and Chinese Influence

Those who are familiar with Vietnamese history point to three "births" of Vietnam. The first birth of Vietnam was during the Dong-son period, estimated sometime around 700 B.C. The second birth of Vietnam resulted from Vietnam gaining independence from China in the tenth century A.D. The final birth is associated with Vietnam's recent overthrow of colonial rule and its establishment once again as an independent nation. Let us begin with a discussion of early Chinese-Vietnamese relations associated with the first birth period to the tenth century.

Very few contemporary nation-states were around in 700 B.C. In the case of Vietnam and China, reasonably detailed written records exist documenting relations with one another. This period is known as prehistory, or Dong-son, for the Vietnamese, though the Chinese were already well into their recorded history. The Chinese had interest in their neighbor for several important reasons. Like any nation-state, the Chinese felt it important not to feel threatened by their neighbors. For the most part, China's foreign relations were conducted with a view to normalizing and nominally controlling political relations with its neighbors in order to enhance domestic stability. The Chinese considered anyone living outside the borders of the middle kingdom to be barbarians. This was not only true for the Mongolians to the north, but for the Koreans in the northeast, and the Vietnamese on their southern border. By the time the Han dynasty was established (circa 200 B.C.), China had more than just a passing interest in Vietnam and sought to establish a firm presence there.[3]

The Chinese wanted to culturize and pacify the "southern barbarians" and sought the abundant riches found in Vietnam.[4] Tributary status was not immediately imposed on Vietnam. The Chinese brought in technologies and traditions that the Vietnamese did not have. But some customs were not readily accepted by the Vietnamese. The Han state was Confucian, and the fiercely independent Vietnamese fought the Confucian and Chinese ways. Despite Vietnamese resistance, it was evident that the Chinese were determined to increase their influence in Vietnam. Finally, the Vietnamese emperor realized that China's superior power was too much to resist and he requested that Vietnam be given status as a tributary state to avoid the danger of Chinese occupation forces entering Vietnam.[5]

The tributary status gradually gave way to more permanent Chinese control. By 111 B.C. the Han dynasty had effectively conquered Nan Yueh (Yue Nan, or Vietnam) by force, which added permanency to the already heavily dominated Chinese region.[6] With the conquering Han came the splendor of that Chinese dynasty. Bronzes, a written language, and other Chinese traditions all entered Vietnam. Within a short time, Vietnam began to function like a Chinese state, reflecting the social structure that was so characteristically Chinese.

> Into such a society came the soldiers and administrators of the world's most advanced civilization, and they carried with them the learning and techniques of China. At first the effects were limited because the Chinese seem to have permitted the indigenous structure of chiefs and headmen to remain in being and to function under overall Chinese control. With the arrival of more and more officials and administrators over the years Chinese rule inevitably became increasingly direct, which led to the growing Sinization of the local people. Vietnamese society developed along the lines of that in China, as did the apparatus of administration employed to govern it. In time Vietnamese scholars began to compete in the Chinese state examinations and to obtain posts in the imperial administration. Vietnam took on the life of a Chinese province, paying taxes to the emperor, governed by officials appointed by the court, studying the Chinese classics, and enjoying peace, order, and stability hitherto unknown.[7]

Despite the overwhelming influence of Han rule over Vietnam, the Vietnamese were able to retain a great deal of their native culture. In the government ranks, the Chinese kept local Vietnamese leaders as prefecture administrators, thus maintaining a local political culture amidst Han rule.[8] Nationalist movements were led by several Vietnamese who rose up against Han armies in an attempt to liberate Vietnam. In most cases the rebellions were met with strong resistance from the occupying Hans and ultimately led to stronger Chinese rule.[9] Inter-marriages occurred between the Han and Viet peoples which strengthened the allegiance of some living in Vietnam toward the Han, but this too ultimately strengthened the trend toward greater Vietnamese nationalism.

In A.D. 40 two sisters surnamed Trung were able to lead a rebellion and restore some territory and government control to the Vietnamese. Taking advantage of weaknesses which developed within the Han court, and with the growing tide of Vietnamese nationalism, the Trung sisters were able to rally support to fight against Han rule. Their example of courage and anti-imperialism has been used many times throughout Vietnamese history to rally the people against foreign influence. In the thirteenth century, Vietnamese historian Le Van Huu wrote:

> Trung Trac and Trung Nhi were women; they gave one shout and all the prefectures of Cuu-chan, Nhat-nam, and Ho-p'u, along with sixty-five strongholds beyond the passes, responded to them, and, establishing the nation, they proclaimed themselves queens as easily as turning over their hands, which shows that our land of Viet was able to establish a royal tradition. What a pity that, for a thousand years after this, the men of our land bowed their heads, folded their arms, and served the northerners; how shameful this is in comparison with the two Trung sisters, who were women! Ah, it is enough to make one want to die![10]

Many of the tactics used by the Trung sisters were typical of great nationalist movements, as they called on the strength of the indigenous culture, traditional religion, art forms, etc. The Trung sisters proclaimed that the ideal Vietnamese ruler should be able to resist the political domination of China and domesticate Chinese culture at the same time. Some scholars argue this was essentially what happened as the two systems seemed to operate alongside each other without the traditional Vietnamese norms suffering too much.[11]

With the decline of the Han dynasty in China some things

became very apparent in Vietnam. During the period A.D. 100 to 400, the Hans in Vietnam had become more "Vietnamized" than the Vietnamese became "Sinocized." Government administrators and others associated with the Han court had come to prefer Vietnamese language and customs more than those of China.[12] After the Han, Chinese rule in Vietnam was sporadic and depended on the strength of the dynasties in China. Taxes were seldom extracted, though riches continued to flow into China from Vietnam with some regularity. The Vietnamese were able to maintain a distinctly Vietnamese life-style, reflected by the strong role of women, and the prevailing sense of law and traditional Vietnamese society. These characteristics of Vietnamese life outlasted the Han, Jin, Sui, Song, Ji, and Tang dynasties.[13]

The Han dynasty was replaced by the Jin dynasty (265–419). But the Jin dynasty did not enjoy the strength and splendor of the Han dynasty, nor did the dynasties that followed the Jin. China's relationship with Vietnam continued on a weak tributary basis. The various governments of China were able to trade more with Vietnam, but were unable to increase significantly tax revenues or take more political control of Vietnam.[14] By the time the Tang had taken over in Vietnam, the people sensed a weakened Chinese position and did not leave the river valleys for the highlands as they had attempted during Han rule. In fact, the people seemed content to remain under dual Vietnamese and Chinese control. Tang power declined in Vietnam, and in China, though the dynasty's influence has been continually criticized by the Vietnamese to this day. With the decline of the Tang court and the rise of Vietnamese nationalism, rebellions occurred frequently and Vietnam set the stage for its second birth, which marked the permanent disposal of Chinese rule.[15]

From the Tenth Century to Colonial Rule

We have seen from the foregoing discussion that Chinese rule over the Vietnamese up to 900 A.D. was not as rigid as some may have supposed. There is no doubt the Chinese were resented in

Table 1.1

Principal Regimes In Vietnam

Regime	Capital	Period
Later Li dynasty	Hanoi	1010–1225
Tran dynasty	Hanoi	1225–1400
Later Le dynasty	Hanoi	1428–1789
Mac dynasty	Hanoi	1527–1592
	Cao-Bang	1592–1677
Trinh family (Tongking)	Hanoi	1539–1787
Nguyen family of Hue	Hue	1558–1777
Tay-son rulers	Saigon, Hue, Hanoi	1788–1802
Nguyen dynasty	Hue	1802–1945

Source: Fairbank, John K., Edwin O. Reischauer, and Albert M. Craig. *East Asia: Tradition and Transformation*, Revised edition. Copyright © 1989 by Houghton Mifflin Co. Used with permission.

Vietnam, but there is also adequate evidence to support the idea that aspects of Vietnamese life that were uniquely Vietnamese remained. In fact, the expansion of Chinese society over Vietnam has been described by some as merely a matter of military-administrative absorption, rather than an imposition of Chinese life on the Vietnamese.[16]

The reason for Vietnam gaining independence by 939 was not because it had overthrown the Chinese, but rather because the Chinese were trying to settle their own internal power struggle. Out of this struggle came the organization of the Sung—a dynasty with little interest in Vietnam. The Vietnamese, therefore, were able to begin their own independent struggle and Ngo Quyen, who had fought the Chinese, became the founder of the first authentic dynasty of Vietnam.[17] He proclaimed the valley areas of the Hue and Red rivers to be Vietnamese territory and thus claimed full independence from China.

But Ngo was unable to maintain control over the people, who quickly lost their allegiance to the emperor and turned their loyalties to Dinh Bo Linh, a peasant who founded the Dinh dynasty. But Dinh was forced to step down after rival landlords had assassinated many of his family members. A period of instability ensued.

Beginning in 1009, stability came to Vietnam. The Ly dynasty lasted for 215 years. This dynasty was able to consolidate power and subdue the ambitions of the various warlords. The Chinese tried to recapture Vietnam in 1057 and several times afterward, but the Vietnamese were able to repel the invasions.

Government in Vietnam closely resembled the Chinese model. Vietnam was divided into provinces, prefectures, and departments. Three-year civil service exams were held to recruit trained civil and military officials.

In 1224, the Tran family began their dynastic rule which lasted until 1400. They proved to be successful in building dikes along the rivers, draining swamps, and continuing to train a powerful military force. This was necessary as not only did they have to worry about the Mongolians who were now conquering China, but they also had to worry about the extreme south (of Vietnam).[18] The Tran-led regime was able to keep the Mongolians from taking over Vietnam because of their firm control and stalwart defense of the Red River valley. But the Mongolians drained the army of Vietnam so that by 1400, the southern population was gaining ground rapidly against the Vietnamese of the North.

By 1400, the Tran dynasty had fallen, and in 1407 the Chinese under the Ming dynasty moved into Vietnam and captured the nation once again. Though short-lived, Ming control over Vietnam was extremely harsh.

> The rule of the Ming was worse than anything the Vietnamese had experienced during previous attempts to make them Chinese. Besides ruthlessly exploiting the country, the Ming rulers took radical measures to denationalize the Vietnamese. Schools were permitted to teach only in Chinese. All local cults were suppressed. What national literature Vietnam had produced was confiscated and shipped to China. The women were forced to wear Chinese dress, the men to wear long hair; in order to tighten control of the people, an identity card was issued to every citizen. After ten years of Ming rule, it was clear to every Vietnamese patriot that the survival of their people, more than ever before, depended on their ability to free themselves from Chinese domination.[19]

The Vietnamese had experienced independence for too long and Ming rule served to strengthen nationalism among them. Slowly at first, then by chain reaction, provinces in Vietnam began resisting the Chinese occupation, so that by 1428 the Chinese left Vietnam and the Le dynasty was born.

The Le dynasty redistributed lands that were held by the Chinese or by Chinese sympathizers. They also established Confucian customs and laws which were borrowed from the Ming, except they gave more rights to female citizens than those afforded to Chinese women.[20] Rulers of the Le established a strong military and moved into areas never before of interest to Vietnam. By 1471, most of the south had been conquered, except for the furthermost tip, and brought under Vietnamese control.[21]

Vietnam did not enjoy the blessings of domestic tranquility from 1500 to the period of colonization. Internal strife was high, corruption among government officials was widespread, and Vietnam had become a place of refuge for Ming loyalists fleeing China. Many of these refugees became civil servants who opened up communication lines between the capital of Vietnam (then at Hue) and Beijing.[22] In addition to these problems, Vietnam was visited by Dominican missionaries in 1527, Portuguese military members in 1535, and Jesuit missionaries in 1615.[23] Proselytizing began in earnest, which resulted in the expulsion of the missionaries in 1645. Within a short time, word had spread to Europe of the wealth found in Vietnam. Gold, rich soil, silk, and spices all aroused the interest of the French and other foreigners. Vietnam voluntarily submitted to the tribute system of China once again in 1788 as part of Vietnamese emperor Gia Long's desire to maintain security and independence from one another. For China, Vietnam's paying tribute was helpful not only for border protection, but as a buffer against further aggression from the West.[24] The tribute system was rigid and marked by distinct rituals:

> a. non-Chinese rulers were given a patent of appointment and an official seal for use in correspondence;

   b. they were given a noble rank in the Ch'ing [Qing] hierarchy;

   c. they dated their communications by the Ch'ing [Qing] calendar;

   d. they presented tribute memorials of various sorts on appropriate statutory occasions;

   e. they also presented a symbolic tribute *(kung)* [*gong*] of local products;

   f. they or their envoys were escorted to court by the imperial post;

   g. they performed the appropriate ceremonies of the Ch'ing [Qing] court, notably the kowtow;

   h. they received imperial gifts in return; and

   i. they were granted certain privileges of trade at the frontier and at the capital.[25]

Between 1803 and 1853, Nguyen rulers sent fourteen missions to Beijing. Their government structure became so Sinicized that their leaders were called sons of heaven and they referred to Cambodians as barbarians. They called their court the Trung Quoc (Zhong guo, or Middle Kingdom, as China did) and exacted tribute from regional rulers within Vietnam and neighboring areas.[26]

Gia Long accepted other aspects of Chinese society as well, recognizing that Chinese culture strengthened his country in ways that most Southeast Asian traditions could not. The influence of Chinese familialization in Vietnam added to the cohesiveness of that society and set it apart from the other cultures in the region. But Vietnam was able to absorb other traditions from Southeast Asia, like warring techniques, which gave Vietnam a degree of independence from China.[27] At the same time, Vietnam was trying to thwart French interests in the region. In 1820 Gia Long appointed Minh Mang as his successor, a move that worried the French because Minh was a devout Confucianist and openly anti-West.[28] He was intelligent and knew far more about the Europeans than did the Qing court in Beijing. Minh Mang was able to renew Vietnam and bring the Vietnamese together in their opposition to the French.

The French were openly bitter over their treatment by Minh

and were happy to see him replaced in 1841 by Thieu Tri. Thieu tried to stop all missionary work from continuing in Vietnam, but French warships and emissaries refused to accept the Vietnamese court's wishes. Finally, Vietnamese resistance to the French fell to the duty of their last emperor, Tu Duc, who was unable to turn events around, culminating in a French invasion in 1857, which marked the end of an independent Vietnam and a Chinese tributary state.

Sino-Vietnamese Relations during the Colonial Era

Vietnam tried to settle its differences with France through diplomatic channels, but these efforts failed. French missionaries made frequent requests for intervention and encouraged an all-out invasion of Vietnam. The Christian missionaries were able to convert over 300,000 Vietnamese by 1825, but local Vietnamese gentry and government officials felt the Confucian system was seriously challenged by western religion. Extermination orders were issued to attack missionaries, which gave the French colonists a reason to intervene.[29] But the invasion of 1857 was prompted more out of concern for the market possibilities in Vietnam than for missionary requests.

The market system was in many respects as alien to the Vietnamese as western religion. Commerce was carried on in Vietnam prior to French influence, but not with the complexity or to the extent that the colonists had envisioned. Capitalism

> appeared to the Vietnamese people, and especially to the educated and politically conscious minority, as a product of foreign rule, to be abolished together with colonialism. This, together with the denial of democracy, explains not only the revolutionary character of Vietnam's anticolonial movement but also why it was easy for so many determined nationalists to embrace Communist ideas.[30]

China also resented foreign rule. Numerous unequal treaties and invasions on Chinese soil angered the Qing court. The Chinese sought to fight against colonialism wherever they felt it was a challenge to their security. Vietnam's fall to colonialism meant the Chinese had to seek ways to harm the French presence in their traditional tribute state to the south. The French were suspicious of this situation and sought to stamp out anything that could be construed as insurgency initiated from China. Colonists tried to stop the use of Chinese characters, fearing that anticolonial literature could be easily distributed among the Vietnamese who were familiar with their neighbor's writing system.[31] Beijing masked its hatred for the French but continued to support the Vietnamese who opposed French rule. Even after the Franco-Chinese treaty of 1887, the Chinese continued to support Vietnamese insurgency, fearing their own security depended on these efforts. China continued to traffic arms throughout the colonial era in an effort to secure its borders and rid the area of western domination.[32]

But historic differences between Vietnam and China continued to surface. The French were able to use effectively the resentment of the Vietnamese against Chinese businessmen to their favor. They acted as peacemakers in the disputes, serving as mediators, which added to their legitimacy in their own minds, and to some extent in the eyes of those involved in the disputes.[33] But the official view from Beijing and the concern of influential Vietnamese was that the French were the main problem.[34]

By 1902, China served as a base for Vietnamese nationalism. Phan Boi Chau, a Vietnamese nationalist leader, met with Sun Yat-sen, the father of modern China, and learned useful revolutionary and propaganda techniques deemed helpful to the Vietnamese and of benefit to China's revolutionary movement as well. In fact, some have argued that Sun Yat-sen believed Vietnam was more important to China's revolution than China to Vietnam's, because Vietnam could keep the French occupied and tire colonial efforts in Asia, and could also serve as a place of refuge for Chinese patriots.[35] In 1907 and 1908, Vietnam did, in fact, serve as a base for Chinese nationalism and temporary refuge, as the various Chinese political factions fell out of grace with one another.[36]

China's internal disagreements over how best to get along with the revolution was stressful to Vietnamese leaders as well. Ho Chi Minh (Nguyen Ai Quoc) was reluctant to ask for Chinese Communist or Chinese Nationalist (Guomindang, or GMD) support against the Japanese, for fear that one or both of them might misunderstand his intents and have him arrested (a frequent problem for Ho in China).[37] Nguyen Ai Quoc had, in fact, changed his name to Ho Chi Minh in an attempt to hide his Vietnamese background while in China to avoid arrest.[38] Despite these efforts, Ho was arrested and spent months in chains in Chinese prisons.

During the CCP (Chinese Communist Party)-GMD alliance of 1940, Phan Boi Chau was able to find cooperation from both factions. He arranged to have forty Vietnamese enroll in Chiang Kai-shek's Whampoa Military Academy. This training proved to be important for the Vietnamese resistance to the French, especially in the attack on Long Son in 1940 (located near the Vietnam-China border).[39] Also during that year, Ho Chi Minh was able to enter into an agreement with the CCP. The most important points of this agreement included:

1. Establishment of a Sino-Vietnamese united front against the Japanese.

2. The Indochinese Communist Party (ICP) would send cadres to Yunnan Province, China, for training in political warfare and propaganda.

3. The CCP would represent the ICP at the Comintern and would give the ICP 50,000 Chinese dollars to carry on revolutionary efforts.[40]

The above agreement seemed to be mostly symbolic as momentum for an Asian communist movement lost ground when the CCP redirected its efforts to carry on with its own revolution. Phan Van Dong, Vo Nguyen Giap, Ho Chi Minh, and others continued to use Yunnan as their launching ground for the resistance movement. In addition, Ho sought financing for the Vietminh who were now taking back substantial ground in Vietnam (1944–45). Ho turned to Washington because he felt the

Americans were more sympathetic to the Vietminh's efforts than others in the West, and likely to give financial and tactical help. This displeased the CCP, which caused the uncertain relationship between the Vietminh and the CCP to worsen.[41] The United States assisted the Vietminh in overthrowing the Japanese puppet government, whereas the CCP offered no help. This left few close friends on Chinese soil for the Vietminh.

The Vietminh couldn't rely on the GMD for assistance at the close of the war either. Many in the GMD preferred the French colonialists to the Vietnamese leadership, due to the Vietminh's communist leanings. In fact, Guomindang forces entered Vietnam after the war, disarmed the Vietnamese, and accepted the Japanese surrender of Vietnam, thus leaving no official acknowledgment of the efforts of the Vietminh during the war. This left Vietnamese leaders to fear that the Chinese were once again planning to occupy Vietnam or at least to demand the resumption of a dependent status.[42] The GMD feared that a Vietnam under the control of the French would mean an ultimate loss of Chinese influence in the region.[43] Ho Chi Minh became convinced in late 1945 that the Chinese had as their objective to fight Vietnam and bring it under Chinese control. He was quoted to have said that it was "Far better to smell the dung of the French than to eat Chinese dung all one's life."[44]

GMD troops marched into Vietnam in October 1945, officially recognized the French colonial rule, and avoided any acknowledgment of the Vietminh. The Vietminh resented the GMD and armed conflict with the conquering GMD quickly followed.[45] By 1946, Ho Chi Minh and the Vietminh were fighting on three different fronts against three different enemies, the French, the Chinese, and the Vietnamese nationalists.[46]

There was little activity between China and Vietnam from 1947 to 1948. The Vietminh felt they were betrayed by the GMD when their nation was turned over once again to the French—an act supervised in part by the Chinese Nationalists. During this time, a few members of the CCP found refuge in Vietnam, once again using it as a place to launch incursions into China. In 1949,

Mao Zedong called on Vietnam to look to the "model" provided by China for revolution. Mao felt that the experience of the Chinese Communists provided a blueprint for other nation-states to follow, particularly other Asian states. Mao's remarks were quickly followed with formal assistance to the Vietminh. Military training and matériel flowed into Vietnam from the Chinese to assist the Vietnamese in ridding their country of the French colonists. Translations of major Marxist writings were made available. Trade and cultural exchanges began on a somewhat regular basis. Propaganda methods were taught to the Vietminh in order to further their influence in areas held by the French or by Vietnamese nationalists.[47]

In the years following 1949, aid from China increased. In 1951 the Chinese had five thousand military advisors in Vietnam, which grew to around eight thousand in 1952. Many of these advisors were officers, including four generals. By 1952, the Chinese had sent in eighty-two thousand tons of military equipment to assist the Vietminh.[48] The Vietminh were enjoying great military and political successes in the areas they held when the Geneva talks got underway in 1954. The French knew they were defeated and expressed the desire common to all western nations—that Vietnam be divided so that the Vietminh could not unify the country.

At the time of the talks the Vietminh were not only busy in Vietnam, but were also directing movements in Laos and Cambodia. Almost all nations present at the Geneva talks voiced concern about the intentions of the Vietminh in the neighboring Southeast Asian countries. The Vietminh denied they were involved in neighboring countries at first, until Zhou Enlai was able to convince Ho Chi Minh that it was in the best interest of the Vietminh to admit their presence in Laos and Cambodia and agree to pull out.[49] This was not an easy decision for Ho to make, for he felt the other Indochinese states would be a boon to Vietnam's security if they too were of a common communist ideology—a point probably understood by the Chinese who held the same position toward Vietnam. It is argued by some that

Zhou Enlai had decided in early 1953 that a negotiated settlement on the issue was especially important to the Chinese. Beijing was worried about western powers increasing their presence in the region if Vietnam continued its drive for an Indochina federation. In addition, Zhou was interested in the prospects for trade with the outside world which would occur if China was not continually supporting Vietnam in a conflict that was defined in cold war terms.[50] Thus Ho Chi Minh did not like the settlement but went along with the divided-nation plan at the infamous seventeenth parallel and agreed to an independent Laos and Cambodia.[51]

The Soviet Union didn't seem to play as an important part in the discussions as the Chinese, though there are indications that the Soviets also favored negotiations with the French. The Soviets had provided matériel, advisors, and training to the Vietnamese in their efforts against the French, and were looking for a way to end these expenses.[52] Zhou Enlai was able to convince the West and the Vietnamese on several occasions of the value of continued negotiation and compromise. Though Ho Chi Minh may have resented the Chinese somewhat for their pressure on the Vietminh to compromise in the talks, he still felt closer to Beijing than to Moscow. At the establishment of the Democratic Republic of Vietnam (DRV, or North Vietnam), Ho sent five high-ranking officials to meet the new ambassador from Beijing at the Sino-Vietnamese border and gave little attention to the new Soviet ambassador.[53]

Zhou Enlai took it upon himself to decide what terms were acceptable for ending the conflict with the French. When it seemed that a negotiated settlement would fall through, Zhou met with French negotiator Pierre Mendes-France in private to discuss the terms acceptable to both France and China. Foremost on Zhou's mind was China's security, particularly since

> the Chinese had just suffered a million casualties in Korea, and the conflict had nearly spilled over their border. Zhou's primary aim at Geneva was to carve out an agreement that would deny the United

States a pretext to intervene in Indochina and again threaten China. Thus he sought a settlement that would keep the French in their former possession, to the exclusion of the Americans.

Such an accommodation inevitably required a sacrifice of the Vietminh's objectives. But Zhou put China's priorities first. Besides, Chinese foreign policy throughout the centuries had been to fragment Southeast Asia in order to influence its states, and Zhou subscribed to that tradition.[54]

Zhou and Mendes-France made the final agreement to end French involvement in the Indochinese conflict. Zhou in turn was able to convince the Vietnamese to go along with the agreement, even though it was completely contrary to their goals for a united Vietnamese nation. In short, the Geneva agreement called for a cessation of military conflict, outlined a plan for a political settlement intended to reunite the nation, and encouraged the Vietminh to speed up talks with the South. On July 20, the agreement was signed with support from the Chinese, the Russians, and the West European powers. The United States agreed not to meddle in the agreement though it was generally not satisfied with it.[55]

Though relations between Hanoi and Beijing seemed to start on a pleasant note, Geneva marked only the beginning of troubles Hanoi would have with a larger communist partner. From 1954 to the present, Hanoi has had to play the Chinese against the Soviets and vice versa in order to set its own foreign and domestic policy objectives.

Between a Rock and a Hard Place:
Hanoi, Beijing, and the Superpowers, 1954–1975

The proceedings and events of the Geneva talks were not to be forgotten by the Vietnamese. The selling out of Vietnamese interests on the part of the Chinese remains a major obstacle in the Sino-Vietnamese conflict today. Events following Geneva continued to anger the Vietnamese. Before returning to Beijing, Zhou Enlai hosted a dinner for all the participants in the Geneva talks. Zhou invited Ngo Dinh Luyen, brother of Ngo Dinh Diem, the infamous South Vietnamese racketeer/dictator. The move infuriated Pham Van Dong who felt betrayed by a communist compatriot inviting a French puppet and archenemy to the dinner. Zhou's intention was to demonstrate that China could live with two Vietnams, and would even prefer a divided Vietnam to one controlled solely by the Vietminh.[56]

Despite his anger and defeat at the Geneva conference, Ho Chi Minh did his best to get along with the Chinese. During this period, Moscow seemed to be more of a risk to forge an alliance with than Beijing was. The Soviets were experiencing major power shifts within the Politburo, in large part due to the vacuum left after Stalin's death. By early 1957, the Soviet Union proposed a permanent partition of Vietnam in the United Nations, by suggesting representation in the international organization by both the North and South Vietnamese governments. Washington rejected the proposal, which saved the Vietminh from a showdown over the issue with Moscow and moved the DRV closer to the Chinese camp.[57] In addition, the Soviet's strong-arm tactics in East Europe sent shock waves throughout the communist world that resulted in a loss of Soviet prestige both within and outside the exaggerated socialist bloc. Finally, the DRV, by virtue of its claiming communist allegiance, was deadlocked into the cold war, whether it wanted to be or not. These circumstances led the Vietnamese Communists to choose the lesser of two evils, which at this time seemed to be the Chinese because they seemed to pose less of a threat.

The Chinese provided training and moral support for the Vietnamese Communists. The Chinese formula of revolution taught to the Vietnamese consisted of three parts: cadre representation, formation of cell units, and self-criticism sessions. The formula had been used extensively by the Chinese Communists and was found to be effective in ridding the country of party enemies. The Vietnamese adopted the system more or less to respect the Chinese, though they held reservations about its effectiveness in their own experience.

The three-level system of organization roughly worked as follows: Cadres, the majority of whom were party members, took charge of making sure the party line was followed by the masses. They were in charge of recruiting talent and organizing day-to-day affairs in local areas. The local inhabitants were organized into cell units with a cadre watching over each unit to make sure party directives were followed and to schedule propaganda sessions to spread the theory of Vietnamese Marxism. Finally, self-criticism sessions were held where the rank-and-file could stand and confess their impure thinking and commit themselves to proper Marxist revolutionary action. Though the Chinese showed strong approval of the three-level system, the Vietnamese were less optimistic and preferred to set their own guidelines for getting on with their revolution.

By the early 1960s, it became obvious to all interested in the fate of Indochina that Washington had more than just a passing interest in the affairs of that region. The United States sent more advisors and more matériel into Vietnam in an attempt to bolster the South Vietnamese government. When Moscow, Beijing, and Hanoi saw Washington's unwavering support for the South, even with the ever-changing nature of South Vietnam's political hierarchy, all doubt was removed as to whether or not the Americans were committed to the South.

When the famous Gulf of Tonkin incident occurred in August of 1964, Khrushchev had already been trying to convince the North to negotiate a settlement for some time. The Hanoi regime was still closer to the Chinese at this time, but the Soviets sent firepower in the form of surface-to-air missiles and other advanced equipment needed to continue the war effort. Soviet assistance forced Hanoi to consider negotiations to appease Moscow. But the ouster of Khrushchev and the events at Tonkin changed the situation and the DRV found itself at war with the United States.[58]

With Washington fully committed to a military settlement of the problems in Vietnam, Mao Zedong began to urge Hanoi to adopt the Chinese method of protracted warfare with the United

States, because he felt it had been so successful in the Chinese communist experience against Chiang Kai-shek's Nationalists in the early days of China's revolution. In late 1964 and early 1965 Mao insisted that protracted war was the answer to counter the superiority of American firepower.[59] China was also in favor of the protracted method of warfare because it was less of a burden to them at a time when tensions were rising on the Sino-Russian border, necessitating the build-up of the Chinese arsenal.[60]

Despite Chinese overtures to change Vietnam's strategy of fighting the war, the Vietnamese still felt that Beijing was a close ally. The new leadership in Moscow in early 1965 sent Aleksei Kosygin to Hanoi to try to convince the DRV to negotiate an end to the war as it was threatening the Soviet Union's peaceful coexistence policy. As an incentive for acceptance of Moscow's offer, aid was promised.[61]

These were not easy days for Hanoi. On the one hand, the DRV had to appease both the Chinese and Russians in order to retain aid and support, and yet it lamented having to bow to the two giants' whims and desires. In an attempt to maintain its own policy interests, Hanoi played the two against each other, giving outward praise to the superiority of protracted war as espoused by Chairman Mao, and claiming that sophisticated weapons supplied by the Russians would improve Hanoi's position at the bargaining table. But while the three communist powers recognized the triangular relationship was not all roses, the United States leadership overestimated the cooperation enjoyed by the three communist powers. Campaigning in 1968, Richard Nixon forwarded his view of communism as a global power seeking world domination. He was not unique in his view, as his predecessors had held similar positions, which meant an ever-growing commitment of American forces, which by late 1968 had grown to 550,000 soldiers.[62]

In 1968 Hanoi's allegiance began to shift toward Moscow. Vietnam was using outposts and territories in Laos and Cambodia to transfer matériel into South Vietnam, and to pacify and strengthen communist movements among its Indochinese neighbors. To Beijing this created two major problems. First, Hanoi was moving ahead with its plans for a rapid reunification of Vietnam, which would mean a strong unified country to the south of China's borders. Second, Vietnam was in a position to influence directly the political direction of the other Indochinese states, which would give the Vietnamese greater power in the Southeast Asia region—a condition Beijing feared almost as much as a direct war with the United States.

Moscow, on the other hand, favored growing Vietnamese influence in the region, as it meant the possibility of greater presence for the Soviets in Southeast Asia, an area where they had no previous experience, plus it added a strategic edge against the Chinese, with whom the Soviets were finding it increasingly difficult to deal on a day-to-day basis. The Chinese objected to the DRV's actions in Indochina, complaining that the United States would surely retaliate against such measures, thus increasing the chances of a larger war in Indochina. Beijing called upon Hanoi to seek ways to negotiate a settlement to the war, a request which Hanoi felt indicated a lack of sensitivity to Vietnamese interests, and a general warming toward Washington.

By 1969 Nixon had in fact expanded operations into Cambodia and Laos which received only casual responses from the Chinese and the Soviets. Henry Kissinger looked at the responses as a marked change in the communist view toward the United States. To Kissinger

> the tempered Chinese and Soviet reactions to our military moves pointed once again to the possibilities of triangular diplomacy to help settle the war. It became unmistakably clear that neither communist power could risk a sharp break with us over Vietnam for fear that we might throw full weight behind the other.[63]

The Cambodian action created new competition between Beijing and Moscow for influence in Indochina. Beijing attempted to block any possibility of Moscow gaining influence in the region, while Moscow saw the region as a strategic prize for use in a new Asian conflict that had gained worldwide attention—the Sino-Soviet border clashes of 1969.

The Sino-Soviet Conflict

As is already evident from the foregoing discussion, a major reason for the growing Hanoi-Beijing rift involved competition for influence in Hanoi between Beijing and Moscow. For this reason, it is necessary to review for a moment the principle factors behind the Sino-Soviet conflict.

When the Chinese and Soviets clashed along the Amur River in March 1969, the world began to evaluate the situation that had led to the conflict between the two communist giants. Most analysts recognized long before the border incidents occurred that relations between Moscow and Beijing had been strained for some time. What was not generally recognized until that time, however, was the intensity of the historical disagreements that had separated China and Russia and had found their way into the modern communist movement.

China's first treaty with a foreign power was with Russia, effected in 1689. This was a direct result of mutual penetration of both nations' territories since 200 B.C. During the period of Western colonialization, the Russians forced the lease of the Liaotung Peninsula, building roads, dams, and coal mines, and would have continued to open the area to industrialization if the Japanese had not taken the area in 1905 after the Russo-Japanese war.[64]

Soviet involvement began in earnest after the founding of the Republic of China in 1911. Sun Yat-sen's Nationalist Party received organizational and logistical assistance from Moscow at an early date—help that continued and largely excluded the CCP until the Chinese civil war ended in 1949. The Chinese Communists were angered by the Soviet acknowledgment of GMD treaties and agreements at the expense of CCP support. The Soviets removed industries they had built in Manchuria, claiming that the treaties governing the industries were negotiated with the GMD, not the CCP who now controlled Manchuria.[65] The Chinese Communists privately complained that while other colonialists had waived their extraterritoriality, the Russians did not, which the Chinese complained was a contradiction of Marxist principles.[66]

Soviet tactics in East Europe, as well as Soviet moves toward India, frightened the Chinese. The war in Indochina further complicated the Beijing-Moscow relationship. Beijing was feeling surrounded by 1969, and Moscow was attempting to strengthen its borders against neighbors on all sides as part of its ongoing policy of geopolitical security. The Chinese took Russian supplies loaded on trains intended for Hanoi in order to bolster their own defenses, actions which eventually caused the Soviets to begin the mass shipping of supplies by ocean and air.[67]

Finally there was the issue of ideology—an issue that clouded all the others. It was difficult then, as it is today, to determine just what role ideology played in the conflict and what position each side was trying to take. At any rate, the rift had grown so great that repeated border clashes occurred off and on during 1969, and threatened the status quo of the entire East Asian region.[68]

The one thing that the Soviets and the Chinese had in common was that by the late 1960s and early 1970s both were tired of Vietnam. China wanted a move toward normalization of relations with the United States, a move that would ultimately cut their costs in support of the DRV's war effort, provide a wedge against the Soviet Union, increase international prestige, and greatly enhance the possibilities toward shaping a clearer direction for China's future. The Soviets, on the other hand, favored an end to the war to cut down on the cost of their commitment to the North Vietnamese.[69]

Negotiating an End to the War

The United States probably exploited the clash between the Soviet Union and China in order to gain points with Beijing. North Vietnamese official Xuan Thuy suspected this of Washington and accused the United States of playing politics in the situation. The argument is well founded: Kissinger admits the situation presented policy makers with options they had previously not enjoyed in the communist world and enabled Washington to make overtures to Zhou Enlai.[70]

Kissinger felt that the Chinese by 1970 were in fact pressuring Hanoi to talk peace with the United States so that Chinese interests could be satisfied. He argues that at the end of 1969 America's

> relationship with the Communist world was slowly becoming trian-gular. We did not consider our opening to China as inherently anti-Soviet. Our objective was to purge our foreign policy of all sentimentality. There was no reason for us to confine our contacts with major Communist countries to the Soviet Union. We moved toward China not to expiate liberal guilt over our China policy of the late 1940s but to shape a global equilibrium. It was not to collude against the Soviet Union but to give us a balancing position to use for constructive ends. . . .[71]

The Vietnamese felt the pressure of international politics interfer-ing with their war. They stepped up efforts to humiliate the United States, believing that domestic turmoil would bleed the Americans of the will to fight and bring victory sooner to the DRV. Chinese overtures to the United States increased, indicating that China had lost its will to continue in Vietnam, fearing the power of a unified Vietnam and of losing an opportunity with the United States.[72] Thus while waging what some considered a proxy war with the United States, contradictory events were occurring during 1971, like "ping-pong diplomacy" and contacts through third parties at diplomatic gatherings in neutral countries. Finally, by 1971 it was obvious that Beijing, Moscow, and Washington had no in-tention of allowing Vietnam to supersede the prospects for indi-vidual national interests. All parties were well on their way to grappling with political realities and not with ideological differ-ences and cold war rhetoric. The events worried Hanoi at a time when it felt victory was at hand.

From Hanoi's perspective the overall situation seemed thus:

1. The United States wants out of Vietnam and is interested in normalizing relations with China and in improving relations with the Soviet Union;

2. The Soviet Union wants a lessened role in Vietnam, while at the same time seeks to improve its position vis-à-vis China and

to improve relations with the United States;

3. The Chinese want to cut back support to Vietnam, obstruct Vietnamese efforts to unify Vietnam and win Indochina, find a wedge against the USSR, normalize relations with the United States, and gain back world recognition after the closed years of the Cultural Revolution;

4. Finally, Hanoi's objectives are to defeat the United States, reunify Vietnam, play the dominant role in Indochina's political future, and walk between Moscow and Beijing in an effort to retain needed support.

With the peace talks in 1972 came the real crunch on Hanoi as they found, to a large extent, they were the only ones fighting for their interests at the bargaining table in Paris. The American negotiators found the Chinese to be sympathetic to U.S. demands in Cambodia. Washington wanted Beijing to use its influence to get the DRV to loosen its hold on Cambodia, but Beijing resisted because of the strain that was already apparent between the two Asian countries. In somewhat of a surprise move, Beijing completely cleared itself of the Paris talks, leaving Hanoi to deal with its own fate.

For the United States, the war in Vietnam seemed to be winding down, although slower than critics had hoped. Washington feared a dry-season offensive would again be in the planning phases by the North Vietnamese. Officials warned Hanoi, and to a lesser extent Beijing and Moscow, that a dry-season offensive would not be greeted with tolerance by the Americans. But Soviet and Chinese influence was waning in Vietnam. Though the two communist giants still wielded considerable influence in Vietnam, it was nothing like the power the two had enjoyed during the 1950s and 1960s. They had more or less resigned themselves to the fact the DRV would in fact launch an offensive, as the Americans had feared.

The April 1972 offensive was supported in theory by both Moscow and Beijing. The offensive presented the opportunity for Moscow and Beijing to try and offset the influence of the other rather than give tacit support for Hanoi's latest venture. In retaliation for the attack, as promised, the United States increased bombing activities against North Vietnam and mined North

Vietnamese harbors. The bombings were, in the eyes of many, the most fierce that had occurred during the entire war. Thousands of bombs were dropped in and around densely populated areas, particularly around the capital of Hanoi. Despite the American air strikes, Beijing and Moscow made little of the situation, which signaled to Washington and Hanoi that the superpowers' agenda would continue despite the war in Vietnam.

Washington had hoped that its bombing activities would especially not damage prospects with Beijing. The Vietnamese clearly did not appreciate the warming up that Moscow and Beijing were enjoying with Washington. In Paris, Le Duc Tho was extremely open when he mentioned how disconcerting it was to have Vietnam's allies seeking improved relations with the United States at the expense of Vietnam's interests. But Kissinger claims Le Duc Tho was most critical of Beijing, foreshadowing that the Chinese were going to lose out to the Soviet Union as the primary influence in Hanoi.[73]

Chinese involvement in Vietnam began to weaken in 1972. It was apparent that Beijing had for the time being resigned itself to the fact that Vietnam was going to carve out its own future regardless of what the Chinese wanted. They made some half-hearted attempts to remain involved. Acting at Richard Nixon's request, the Chinese tried to convince Hanoi to step up efforts to reach an agreement at the peace talks—a move that surely angered the Vietnamese.[74] The Chinese had grown tired of dealing with Hanoi and preferred to get along with their own foreign policy objectives. Kissinger mentions that before and during the peace talks of 1973, Zhou had become so tired of the Vietnam conflict that his way of dealing with Vietnam, Laos, and Cambodia was not to deal with them at all. China feared the inevitable Indochinese-Vietnamese state on its borders, but felt it could do nothing under the circumstances to change the course of events.[75]

Both the Chinese and the Soviets knew it was only a matter of time before the Paris peace accords would be signed. The winding-down of the war between the United States and Vietnam also meant the communist powers were able to go forward with their plans to improve relations with the United States. The Vietnamese were again angered by the warm receptions both the Soviets and the Chinese had given Nixon when he visited their respective capitals. Angry commentaries were published in the official Vietnamese communist newspaper, *Nhan Dan*, criticizing the "communist giants' . . . concern for their immediate and narrow interests was a betrayal of their lofty international duties and would damage the world revolutionary movement."[76]

The ending of the Vietnam War for the United States marked the beginning of yet another Indochinese war. Both Beijing and Moscow knew it was only a matter of time before Saigon and the rest of South Vietnam would fall and Vietnam would be reunited. As a result, the two giants began to consider what future role they were going to play in Indochina and tried to grapple for influence. In November 1974 the stage was set for continued hostility in Southeast Asia—Cambodia in particular, as the USSR recognized the government of Lon Nol, and the PRC recognized the Khmer Rouge. There were no warm feelings on the part of either the USSR for the Lon Nol government or the PRC for the Khmer Rouge, other than they suited the immediate purposes of each of the respective powers. Lon Nol was vehemently anti-Chinese, which provided the Soviets with an added edge against China. The Khmer Rouge were anti-Vietnamese and anti-Soviet, which suited well Chinese interests in the region. But the communist power play in Indochina would eventually bring not just the Khmer Rouge to war with Vietnam, but would also result in a renewal of armed conflict between Vietnam and China in the years to come.

With the help of fresh Soviet assistance to the North, Saigon fell in April 1975 and the DRV succeeded in reuniting Vietnam. The long war which began back in the 1930s had finally ended. For the Vietnamese and the Russians, the capture of Saigon marked a triumphal victory over the western powers and the establishment of a lasting communist presence in Southeast Asia. The Chinese, sensing that the DRV's victory meant trouble for China, were less enthusiastic over the military victory. On the one hand, the Chinese were forced to offer hearty congratulations on Hanoi's victory over the South because of the support they had given the DRV over the years. On the other hand, they played down the victory and tried to promote the idea of a power-sharing compromise with members of the Provisional Revolutionary Government (PRG) who represented many of the guerrilla fighters and other Vietnamese communist groups not giving full allegiance to the DRV. At a dinner celebration in April 1975, Chinese Politburo member Li Xiannian announced to PRG government officials, not the government of the DRV, that the PRC had a ship loaded with food and medicine ready to send to Vietnam. It was obvious to all present that the Chinese preferred the prospects of the PRG ruling Vietnam to the DRV government whom they feared would seek to dominate all of Indochina and forge close links with the Soviet Union at the expense of China's security interests.[77]

During the remainder of 1975, Vietnam sought to fuse closer links to the Soviet Union. There are a number of reasons for this, but historical antagonism, prospects for economic aid, and tensions with the United States left the Vietnamese with little choice but to align closely with the Soviets.[78]

But in considering the current dilemma, the Vietnamese position vis-à-vis China does not differ greatly from what it has been historically. Despite allegiance to communism, and the complexities and opportunities of modern society, Vietnam and China are again at odds with each other. The Vietnamese agenda maintains that Vietnam is only secure with an Indochina sympathetic to Vietnamese political needs. The Chinese feel secure only with a weak or contained Vietnam on its border and therefore consider the Vietnamese problem almost as a pressing domestic concern rather than simply a foreign policy challenge.

Most conflicts begin with a simple or straightforward problem and get complicated as other factors figure in. This is true with the Sino-Vietnamese conflict. Now we turn to a consideration of these intricacies and investigate how they led to the 1979 war between China and Vietnam.

2

Beijing, Hanoi, and Indochina— Steps to the Clash

Without a doubt, the most serious issue dividing Vietnam and China has been the struggle for dominance in Indochina. Chapters two, three, and four are devoted to sorting out the competing policies Beijing and Hanoi have supported to try to secure a presence in Indochina. In the present chapter this competition will be analyzed from 1975 to the end of the 1979 war between China and Vietnam. The issues here are complex as they involve consideration of other regional actors as well, namely Cambodia, Laos, and the Association of Southeast Asian Nations (ASEAN).

The first section will look at the initial strains between China and Vietnam that emerged in 1975. This will be followed by a discussion of the growing instability within the Indochina region after 1975 and how Beijing and Hanoi reacted to these events. The third section looks at the Vietnamese invasion of Cambodia and the subsequent Chinese invasion of Vietnam. A summary and conclusion will follow.

China and Vietnam 1975: "Friends" Dig Up Their Differences

Many outside observers were interested to see how Beijing would react to the takeover of South Vietnam by Hanoi. There had been wide speculation that China preferred a divided Vietnam because it feared what effect a united Vietnam might have on the rest of Indochina. When Hanoi's victory over the South was officially announced, it took the New China News Agency (NCNA) seven hours to report the event, and even then it was a subdued response. Reports began to circulate immediately that Hanoi and Beijing were experiencing problems as Western diplomats did not hear Hanoi authorities even mention China by name for two weeks following the victory.

After a few days, the Chinese issued a second news release on the DRV's victory, frankly congratulating the Vietnamese, and then emphasizing the need for an independent Laos and Cambodia—in other words, a direct warning to Hanoi not to act on any ambitions it may have had to intervene in the neighboring states.[1]

Chinese worries over what Hanoi might have in store for Indochina were well founded. The Vietnamese considered themselves to be the cornerstone of Indochina's communist movement since the early days of the Indochina Communist Party, when they dominated the ranks of the party's membership. Before and after World War II, Vietnam supported insurgency movements in Laos and Cambodia. During the Geneva conference in 1954, Vietnam was forced to give in to Chinese demands to stop insurgency movements in neighboring countries in order to agree to a cease fire with France. In the late 1960s and early 1970s, elements within Laos and Cambodia were considered marginally involved in the war against the United States because their countries contained several supply routes and bases used by the North Vietnamese Army (NVA). Thus Hanoi had a long history of involvement with its Indochina neighbors.

Against this backdrop, Beijing believed Hanoi faced principally two options in Indochina:

1. Drop any ambitions in Indochina and work exclusively on socialist construction at home. This option, Beijing believed, was improbable due to the continued interest Hanoi had shown in its neighbors even at the expense of angering China.

2. Continue to seek greater influence in Indochina and pro-

mote socialist construction at home, while seeking continued economic and political support from Moscow and Beijing. Despite the danger of seriously harming the relationship between Vietnam and China, this option seemed more likely to Beijing, considering the past ambitions of the Vietnamese in the area and the historical differences that separated Vietnam and China. It is also the option from which China believed it had the most to lose, for not only did it represent an overall gain in influence for Hanoi in the region, it would also receive enthusiastic support from Moscow, which could gain from having a close ally contain China's southern borders.

Hanoi's fears of Chinese ambitions in Indochina were also well founded. The Chinese always seemed to give the Vietnamese support in its struggles against the French and Americans, but that support weakened during both the Geneva talks in 1954 and the Paris talks in 1973. Additionally, Beijing had never taken the communist movements in Indochina seriously, until the PRC was officially born in 1949. At that point, the Chinese sought to control the scope and methods to handle the individual revolutions of the Indochinese states. To the Vietnamese, China was playing out the same role the Chinese had played in past centuries, despite Beijing's self-claimed allegiance of cooperation with its fraternal socialist neighbor Vietnam.

In short, Hanoi viewed China as the principal threat to not just Indochina, but to Vietnam itself, and believed Beijing's goals to be as follows:

1. Beijing will try to establish relations with both the Provisional Revolutionary Government (PRG) of Vietnam, and continue contacts with the Hanoi government, in order to stall the unification of Vietnam.[2]

2. Beijing will seek to extend China's influence into Laos and Cambodia to offset the influence of Vietnam. This not only ensures friendly neighbors, but contains Vietnamese ambitions and limits Soviet influence in the region.

3. Beijing will find ways to pull Hanoi away from the Soviet camp and align it more closely with Beijing in the Sino-Soviet

dispute. This is a long-term goal, but nevertheless important to Beijing.

With Chinese and Vietnamese views conflicting so sharply over Indochina, it is understandable why Hanoi and Beijing responded to each other the way they did at the time of the communist victory over South Vietnam in April 1975. For the remainder of 1975 and 1976, Hanoi and Beijing were cautious toward one another, but remained determined to make their wishes known to one another.

In June 1975, the PRC sent a ship loaded with relief supplies to Da Nang, Vietnam. The ship was not permitted to enter the harbor and therefore remained offshore waiting for instructions. A few days later a Soviet ship approached the harbor and asked if it could enter and deliver its goods. Vietnamese officials responded by telling the Chinese ship to enter the harbor and the Soviet ship followed behind. The following day a public announcement was made by the Vietnamese stating that the USSR was the first country to send aid to Vietnam after its victory. The incident, of course, angered the Chinese.[3]

Further indications of strain surfaced in August when a Vietnamese economic delegation was received coolly by Beijing officials. Communist Chinese sources in Hong Kong believed that the reserved reception was the result of Vietnam's lack of gratitude for Chinese wartime aid, closer ties between Hanoi and Moscow, and competition for influence in Phnom Penh between Hanoi and Beijing.[4] A document released by Beijing in 1978 sheds further light on the incident. Supposedly Zhou Enlai told the Vietnamese economic delegation that China "needed a rest" from giving aid in order to regain strength in the Chinese economy.[5] The Vietnamese delegation left Beijing and went directly to Moscow where they received a warmer reception and a generous aid package.

In 1976, U.S. State Department officials received information that shipments of aid from China to Cambodia via Vietnam were held up in Vietnamese ports by officials demanding that half of the goods be unloaded in Vietnam. The Chinese were angry with the Vietnamese, but went ahead and unloaded the goods. The Chinese stated they chose not to publish these accounts in either the Chinese or outside press in order to prevent a further strain on relations.[6] The Vietnamese actions reflected not just demands for further aid, but a reduction in the aid the Chinese were giving Cambodia. Relations between the SRV and PRC continued their downward spin. In April 1976, reports began to circulate that some fighting had occurred along the Sino-Vietnamese border. The reports indicated that the SRV and the PRC agreed to enter peace talks. The Chinese wanted the talks to encompass also the Cambodian issue that divided Vietnam and China, a point the SRV flatly rejected because Hanoi said the problems in Cambodia would cloud the real issue which only involved Vietnam and China.[7]

Despite the wide and varied reports mentioned above, both sides seemed uncertain about the state of Sino-Vietnamese relations in 1976. It is obvious that Hanoi and Beijing were trying to come to terms with this problem, as neither side was willing to express open dissatisfaction with the other. But Hanoi's leanings toward Moscow increased China's suspicions of the Soviet Union. China viewed Soviet moves toward Vietnam in terms similar to Soviet actions in East Europe. Because the Soviet Union was China's chief adversary, a close alliance with China's chief rival in Asia was indicative of growing Soviet influence worldwide and in particular of a further attempt to contain China. Beijing believed that such geopolitical hegemonism on the part of the Soviets must not be allowed to succeed in Southeast Asia.[8]

The rapid pace of growing relations between Hanoi and Moscow was met with tough talk from Beijing, though it was principally directed toward Moscow. China accused the Soviets of expansion in Southeast Asia and of harboring ambitions to take over the Third World. Though Moscow received the brunt of the criticism, most outside observers recognized that the criticism was meant for both the Vietnamese and the Soviets.[9] The criticism failed to reverse the steady pace of Vietnam-Soviet cooperation and instead was matched by Soviet accusations of Chinese hegemonism in the Indochina region.[10]

In July 1976, PRC ambassador to Hanoi Sun Hao admitted that the relationship between the PRC and the SRV was not as close as China would like. Sun said this was principally because of the apparent closeness between Vietnam and Moscow, but believed it would be short-lived because of the overarching Vietnamese desire for independence. He also admitted that some historical differences between China and Vietnam had resurfaced and that there was a difference as to what was considered to be an acceptable military balance in Asia.[11] Implicit in this argument is a continuing controversy over the fate of Indochina and who should play the dominant role in its future.

Toward the end of 1976, Hanoi and Beijing still considered each other to be the main obstacle to increasing each's interests in Indochina. Though both had competed rigorously for influence in Indochina, little is known about how this competition took place, other than through aid projects and some support for insurgency movements, suggesting that both Vietnam and China were practicing restraint in order to avoid revealing open differences in objectives. In addition, few Southeast Asian countries seemed overly concerned about events in Indochina. Thailand was the exception to this, as it borders Cambodia and Laos and had been suspicious of both Chinese and Vietnamese intentions in the region for decades.[12]

In December a major event transpired which seemed to indicate a serious turn in Sino-Vietnamese relations. At the fourth Party congress in Hanoi, Politburo member Hoang Van Hoan, a pro-Beijing official, was dropped as a ranking member of the Politburo. Also purged were other influential party members considered part of a faction sympathetic to Chinese policies generally and specifically critical of Moscow's role in Vietnamese politics. The purge was considered a major victory for the pro-Soviet faction of the party and marked the most serious shift away from China since the close of the Vietnam war in 1975.[13] Vietnam also moved further from China after the death of Zhou Enlai. Zhou's death left a power struggle within the communist party of China. While Beijing was settling its internal dispute,

Vietnam was able to secure aid from Moscow. Upon hearing the news that Hanoi's aid request was approved by Moscow VCP secretary Le Duan proclaimed the Soviet Union to be "the mightiest socialist state."[14] China, meanwhile, continued to criticize "Soviet social-imperialism and hegemony" and called on the Soviets to stay out of the affairs of Laos, Cambodia, and Vietnam.[15]

The Hanoi shift toward Moscow came at a time when the Chinese and Vietnamese were completing several joint industrial projects which had been started several years earlier. Though Beijing issued a celebratory message on their completion, no indication was given that new projects were in the planning stages.[16] With a pro-Soviet tilt in the Politburo, aid would most likely be coming from Moscow, and Beijing would forgo any consideration of future projects. Hanoi still held hopes that money would be forthcoming from the United States.

When Vietnam was officially reunited in 1975, Hanoi began to assess its chances for relations with the United States. Despite having fought a bitter war with the Americans, Hanoi began to make overtures to Washington. It was clear that Hanoi needed the United States for several important reasons:

1. Vietnam needed economic help. Years of war and seclusion had left the Vietnamese economy seriously disjointed and weak. With the possibilities of aid, Hanoi could begin to rebuild and save its faltering economy. Without American help Vietnam would be forced further into the Soviet camp for assistance, something Hanoi wanted to avoid.

2. Relations with Washington might shelter Vietnam generally from having to walk so carefully between Moscow and Beijing. Although it was clear that Hanoi was closer to Moscow in 1975 than to Beijing, Hanoi preferred to be as independent as possible. Relations and assistance from the United States might help Vietnam's move toward independence.

3. With normal relations between Hanoi and Washington, other countries would most likely be more willing to assist Vietnam. One of the benefits of normalizing relations with Washington was that there was a greater possibility that countries

following Washington's lead would provide financial assistance to the faltering economy.

4. Finally, U.S. recognition might provide Vietnam with a minor buffer against the Chinese, thus holding them at bay and allowing Hanoi greater freedom to follow its own agenda in Indochina. U.S. recognition would acknowledge the reality of a Hanoi-influenced Indochina and serve to prevent Chinese intervention in the region.

Beijing, on the other hand, sought other goals from normalization of relations with the United States. Some of these naturally conflicted with Hanoi's interests:

1. A better relationship with Washington would provide an edge against the Soviets. Any gain of American influence would be considered a net loss for the growing Soviet presence in Asia, and Indochina in particular.

2. An improvement in U.S.-China relations might discourage Vietnam from seeking hegemony in Indochina. The move might undermine any intentions Hanoi had in Indochina, as the United States and China would be allied against Vietnamese expansion.

3. China could benefit from the trade opportunities that would follow normalizing relations with the United States. This would undoubtedly open up China's trade potential with other countries which would follow Washington's lead.

4. Finally, improved relations with Washington would increase China's importance as a world power. Ties with the United States would give Beijing a freer voice to express its opinions over other issues directly affecting China and world political issues generally.

Summary

In 1975 and 1976, differences clearly emerged between Beijing and Hanoi. There is no doubt that these differences had major implications on the relationship before the North Vietnamese victory over the South in 1975, but Hanoi's victory placed new emphasis on these areas of conflict. Though both the Chinese and

Vietnamese remained guarded in their response to one another, it was evident that competing policies in Southeast Asia were clashing, driving the two nations further apart than they had been since Vietnam's drive for independence early in this century. This division began to surface in 1977.

Indochina in Disarray

For a period following the purge of the "pro-China faction" of the Vietnam Communist Party, both the Chinese and Vietnamese continued their cautious approach toward one another. Though public pronouncements contained their usual superficial gestures of goodwill, celebrating the "socialist fraternal unity of nations of which Vietnam and China are a part," official contacts between leaders were much cooler.

In April 1977, Premier Pham Van Dong of the SRV visited Beijing to request aid from the Chinese leadership. This meeting was held with Hua Guofeng, Chen Xilian, and Li Xiannian. A memorandum of the meeting was written by Li Xiannian and sent to Pham Van Dong on June 10, 1977.[17] The memorandum reveals that the talks were tense and heated. China's two major concerns specifically mentioned in the memo are summarized below:

1. China was irritated at the Vietnamese-Soviet rapprochement. In particular, Beijing expressed deep resentment at Vietnam's admission of working with the Soviets to lessen China's regional influence in Southeast Asia.

2. Beijing claimed Vietnam was using historical problems that separated Vietnam and China to incite a new anti-China campaign. Beijing stated that past aggression on the part of various dynasties of China were the acts of feudal leaders and did not reflect the desires of the Chinese Communist Party. Thus the resurgence of animosities between the governments of Vietnam and China were a result of Vietnam's campaign and had nothing to do with the Chinese Communist Party.

The memo did not explicitly mention the differences that separated Vietnam and China over Indochina. This may have been because the political situation in Cambodia had not yet solidified. For the most part, China and Vietnam knew they were at odds over the issue, but tried to keep this division from leading the two nations toward open violence. It is helpful at this point to review the situation of the various countries of Indochina in mid-1977 to see where China and Vietnam differed in their approaches to the region.

Cambodia

Cambodia had been invaded numerous times by the Vietnamese and the Thais. Resentment toward the Vietnamese (and Thais) was thus deep-seated among most Cambodians. In this century, the Vietnamese have received the bulk of Cambodian distrust due to what Cambodia sees as Vietnam's continued efforts to dominate Cambodia by taking the lead in Cambodia's revolutionary movements, and holding land along the Vietnamese border that Cambodians consider properly theirs.

Vietnamese influence in Cambodia was also felt at the grassroots level of society. In 1952 it was estimated that 75 percent of the Khmer population was in debt to moneylenders, most of whom were Vietnamese landlords (some Chinese were also involved).[18] This made the Vietnamese popular targets for Cambodian nationalists. The Khmer Rouge, an extreme arm of the Cambodian Communist Party (KCP), represented most of the rural population, as it was decidedly anti-Vietnamese, anti-West, and extremely pro-Cambodian self-reliance.

The Khmer Rouge were relatively powerless until the United States began bombing missions in Cambodia in 1969 in retaliation for the KCP giving support to Hanoi's war effort. The bombings gave rise to popular support for the Khmer Rouge, who saw Phnom Penh's cooperation with Washington as an abandonment of Cambodia's independence, and viewed the Vietnamese relationship with the KCP as another version of Vietnam's attempts to bring the Khmer people under Vietnamese domination.[19]

In late 1975 the political situation in Cambodia began to change significantly. Prince Norodom Sihanouk fell out of power and the KCP gained complete control of affairs in Phnom Penh. The secretary of the KCP was Pol Pot (previously known as Saloth Sar), recognized as the real power behind the Khmer Rouge. Two of his deputies, Ieng Sary, a brother-in-law of Pol Pot, and Son Sen, were considered to be close associates of Pol Pot and shared Pot's anti-Vietnamese sentiment and pro-China allegiance. The fourth figure in the party leadership was Khieu Samphan, considered to be only marginally important and relatively powerless compared to the other three leaders.[20]

Beijing played up to Pol Pot and the extremists of the Khmer Rouge of Cambodia more because of their anti-Soviet stand and confirmed dislike for Vietnam. Hanoi was decidedly anti–Khmer Rouge, though not anti-KCP. It felt that elements existed in the KCP that favored ties and cooperation with Vietnam and therefore it tried various options to swing the political pendulum in Phnom Penh toward more pro-Hanoi elements.

Laos

Like the Vietnamese, the Laotians had tried to strike a delicate balance between Moscow and Beijing. Unlike Vietnam, however, this balancing act also included distancing Laos as much as possible from Hanoi.[21] Hanoi's troops had been in the Laotian capital of Vientiane since 1961.[22] Unlike the Cambodians, the Laotians aligned with Hanoi in the early 1960s, receiving training and financial support from Vietnam and generally trying to distance themselves from the Chinese who had held tributary relations with Laos for hundreds of years.

When the Vietnamese succeeded in their reunification efforts in 1976, Vientiane criticized Beijing for exerting undue pressure on Hanoi to comply with Beijing's desires. Though much of the rhetoric was intended to prove its allegiance to Hanoi, the statements were nevertheless reluctantly made because they represented the dissolution of Laotian neutrality and forced Vientiane deeper into the political stranglehold of Vietnam. As a result, PRC engineer troops stationed in Laos were recalled.[23]

As Laos continued to drift further away from Beijing, Vientiane moved markedly closer to Hanoi and Moscow. The Laotians did request aid from Beijing in early 1977, but the request was rejected by Hua Guofeng on grounds that Laos was too close to the Soviet Union and Vietnam.[24] In July of that year, the SRV and Laos concluded their Treaty of Friendship and Cooperation pledging to

> carry out a close cooperation aimed at reinforcing the defense capacity, preserving independence, sovereignty and territorial integrity, and defending the people's peaceful labor, against all schemes and acts of sabotage by imperialism and foreign reactionary forces.[25]

The Chinese knew that the above clause was intended to finalize the Laos-Vietnamese friendship at the expense of Chinese interests. Thus Laos was considered by Beijing to be securely entrenched in Hanoi's strategic sphere—a factor that made Cambodia the battleground for China to halt Vietnamese success in Indochina.

Thailand

Thailand tried to remain neutral on the issue for as long as it could. Border problems with the Khmer Rouge brought it close to all-out war with Cambodia on several occasions in the mid-1970s. Bangkok wanted Phnom Penh to remain noncommunist, but when this failed the Thais hoped that the government in power would be responsive to what Bangkok perceived as a Vietnamese threat to all of Indochina. Though Pol Pot's regime shared Bangkok's distrust for the Vietnamese, Thailand was not much better in Pot's mind and border problems grew between the KR and the Thais.

In 1976 Beijing and Bangkok normalized relations, a move many outside observers believed was brought about primarily out of a mutual distrust for Hanoi than for any other reason.[26] As growing tension in the region continued, Bangkok agreed to normalize relations with Hanoi in 1977 in hopes that Vietnam would consider newly forged relations with Thailand before trying any desperate attempts to take control of Cambodia.

From War of Words to Open Hostility

Against this political backdrop, Beijing sought to strengthen its ties with the Pol Pot regime. Pot attended the October first celebrations in Beijing and was received warmly by Chinese authorities. The result of the contact was a direct message to the Vietnamese as to where China stood in terms of the border disagreements separating Vietnam and Cambodia, and more importantly, committed China to seek more direct ways to meet the Vietnamese challenge in Indochina.[27]

The strained relationship between China and Vietnam was becoming more and more apparent to outside observers. When food aid to Vietnam was all but stopped in late 1977, Le Duan commented to reporters on the drastic reduction of support from China, indicating that China's and Vietnam's interests diverged, which limited cooperation on issues such as aid:

> During our anti-U.S. resistance, fraternal countries helped us by giving us weapons and food. By so doing they promoted interests, ensured the survival of socialism and fulfilled their international duties. But during the construction period, aid will be cooperation on the basis of mutual interest.[28]

The Vietnamese had publicly praised the Soviet Union for being the primary provider of aid in the past to Vietnam, but failed to mention China's contributions.[29] Though China's aid to Vietnam was significantly less than that of the Soviet Union, the Chinese still gave more aid to Vietnam than to any other country to which Beijing pledged support. For this reason, Hanoi's failure to mention Chinese aid had a chilling effect on relations, as

China complained that Vietnam was insensitive and ungrateful to China for assistance rendered to the Vietnamese.[30]

In November 1977, a Vietnamese delegation visited Beijing, making perhaps the last public attempt to show goodwill between China and Vietnam. In his speech at a banquet held for the delegation, Hua Guofeng proclaimed that China would "strengthen unity with other socialist countries . . . and ally with all countries subjected to imperialism, and social-imperialist aggressions, subversion, interference, control or bullying . . . .[31] There is no doubt the primary target of Hua's remarks was the Soviet Union. But Vietnamese reliance on the Soviets for financial and political support was great at this time, making the message equally directed at Vietnamese efforts in Cambodia. Le Duan's speech at the banquet served to express Vietnamese interests in continued involvement in Indochina:

> The Vietnamese people have no more earnest desire than to live in peace, to promote and strengthen relations of friendship and cooperation with all countries, and to contribute to the defence of the peace in Southeast Asia and the world, at the same time, we are determined not to allow any imperialism and reactionary force whatsoever to encroach upon our independence and freedom.[32]

In December, Beijing published accounts of Khmer Rouge efforts to defend themselves against foreign aggression from Vietnam. It was one of the first public attempts by China to direct blame for the Cambodia-Vietnam border conflict in Hanoi's direction.[33] At the same time, foreign press services reported Beijing was sending arms to Phnom Penh to resist Vietnamese forces at the border and to stave off Vietnamese intentions to invade.[34] Within a few days, several Chinese advisors who were working with Cambodian forces were captured by the Vietnamese and Premier Dong hinted to members of the press that Cambodia's strength was a result of Sino-U.S. collusion against Vietnam.[35] Some Chinese officials commented to members of the press corps in late January 1978 that responsibility for the war in Cambodia should be clearly directed at Vietnam.[36]

As the winter months passed, the fighting between Vietnam

and Cambodia became fiercer. (Winter is the dry season in Indochina, thus military operations are more easily carried out than during the wet season.) Both Vietnam and Cambodia made sporadic incursions into each other's territory. Despite Cambodia's comparatively weak military, Phnom Penh believed that aggression against the SRV might discourage the SRV from trying to dominate Cambodia.[37] KR troops thus launched a raid into Vietnamese territories despite limited resources—a move that surprised many regional leaders.

Hanoi believed Cambodia was the key in the Indochina balance of power. Thus victory over Cambodia would maximize Hanoi's independence from China (and possibly Moscow), and could greatly increase Vietnam's influence in the entire Southeast Asia region.[38]

As conflict between Cambodia and Vietnam wore on, growing tension between Vietnam and China also reached crisis proportions. Policies directed against Chinese residents living in Vietnam were implemented by Hanoi. Thousands of ethnic Chinese began fleeing Vietnam for China and other Asian countries as rumors of an inevitable China-Vietnam war spread rapidly. Old border and territorial problems that divided China and Vietnam became the focus of threats and counterthreats between Hanoi and Beijing. China severed remaining aid packages and removed all advisors serving in Vietnam. Beijing also closed Vietnamese consulates in Kunming, Guangzhou, and Nanning. The diplomatic battle forced Hanoi deeper into the Soviet sphere.

As the war of words continued between China and Vietnam, the focus began to shift to exposing the other side's designs in Indochina. Hanoi accused Beijing of giving "all-out support for the Kampuchean authorities to conduct a war of aggression committing innumerable barbarous crimes against the Vietnamese people." It further accused China of using other issues to cloud China's real intent which was to "force Vietnam to give up its correct line of independence, sovereignty, and international solidarity."[39] A secret document was published by the SRV foreign ministry in June 1978, which detailed what Hanoi viewed as

China's strategy in Indochina. The principal Vietnamese observations were:

1. China has historically tried to weaken Vietnam in the international community. This is evident from its efforts to divide Vietnam at the Geneva conference in 1954 and to slow reunification in the 1970s.

2. China has tried to limit Vietnamese influence in Laos and Cambodia by supporting those regimes that have opposed Vietnam and Vietnam's struggle for independence.

3. The Chinese authorities would like to topple the current government of Vietnam in order to bring it under Chinese control.

4. China wants to control the destiny of Southeast Asia generally, and views Vietnam and the Soviet Union as a threat to these designs.[40]

China's perceptions of Vietnam mirrored Hanoi's view of China in many respects. Speaking to a British House of Lords delegation, Li Xiannian said that the primary reason Vietnam turned against China was because Vietnam wanted to create an Indochina federation by turning Laos and Cambodia into colonies. Li claimed the PRC had known this for some time and had made China's opposition to the policy known to Hanoi, though China did not go public with the accusation.[41]

In mid-summer, Vietnam was admitted into the Moscow-based economic organization CMEA or COMECON. The admission allowed Vietnam greater access to aid and technical help and filled vacancies left by Chinese technicians who were recalled by Beijing as Vietnam-China ties worsened.[42] It also marked an increase in Vietnam's reliance on the Soviet Union. As a member of CMEA, Vietnam was obliged to consider Moscow first in its dealings with other socialist nations.

Tensions by late summer seemed to lessen somewhat. Most observers considered the Cambodian situation to be stalemated, with Vietnam and China fighting a proxy war.[43] Along with general economic assistance provided by CMEA came weapons from the Soviet Union. The shipments of Soviet arms to Vietnam were far more than the amounts needed to maintain Vietnam's efforts in Cambodia. Chinese authorities expressed the belief that the Soviet Union was arming and encouraging Vietnamese officials to bring China into a border war with Vietnam.[44]

As attention to refugee issues and border incidents seemed to decrease in the Chinese press, more attention was given to Hanoi and Moscow's intentions in Cambodia. The *Renmin ribao* (People's Daily) carried an article calling Vietnam "a junior partner of the Soviet Union" which receives "prodding and support from the Kremlin in whatever it does or says." Referring to the Soviets as "social-imperialists," the article continues:

> Social-imperialism is a past master in conjuring up a "peoples insurgence" as a pretext for invading and subverting a sovereign state. The Vietnamese authorities are well-versed in this trick and have been playing it all along. . . . Moscow and Hanoi are bent on strangling the new-born Kampuchea in its cradle . . . both Hanoi and Moscow are determined to destroy Kampuchea.[45]

But the signing of the Treaty of Friendship and Cooperation between the Soviet Union and Vietnam in early November once again raised anxieties in the region. China saw Article Six of the treaty as a Vietnamese and Soviet attempt to threaten China so that the two signatories' goals in Indochina would not be thwarted by the Chinese:

> In case either party is attacked or threatened with attack, the two parties signatory to the treaty shall immediately consult each other with a view to eliminating that threat, and shall take appropriate and effective measures to safeguard peace and the security of the two countries.[46]

Vice-Premier Deng Xiaoping pointed out at a press conference in Bangkok that the treaty was a component part of the global strategy of the Soviet Union and the "Cuba of Asia" (referring to Vietnam), and that the treaty had a "military nature." Deng argued that the treaty would enable Vietnam to increase its hegemonistic acts as the "Cuba of the East":

> Everybody knows what Cuba is like. We cannot but keep vigilant attention on the Cuba of the East. As for the answer to this question, it depends on how far Vietnam will go. First of all, to what extent it will carry on with its aggression against Kampuchea. We will decide on the way of dealing with it in accordance with the distance it will go with its policy of hegemonism.[47]

Despite the signing of the treaty, Vietnam and the Soviet Union were not as close as some may have believed. Vietnamese officials were open in their assessment of the Soviet Union. One official told an American diplomat that the SRV survived French colonialism and American imperialism, and they would also "survive a Russian friendship."[48] The Soviets were well aware of Vietnam's resentment toward them. A U.S. Department of State official, in summarizing a conversation with a Soviet diplomat, reported the Soviets to be frustrated with Vietnam because they only had a "ten percent" familiarity with what the Vietnamese leadership was thinking.[49]

On December 3, 1978, the Kampuchean National United Front for National Salvation (KNUFNS), under Heng Samrin, was organized. The goal of the KNUFNS was the overthrow of Pol Pot and the establishment of a new socialist regime. Heng Samrin was a Cambodian and former member of the executive committee of the KCP. He had led a revolt against Pol Pot in May 1978. The Vietnamese intended to use Heng Samrin to legitimize their policies in Cambodia. It was thought that if they threw their support behind Samrin, Hanoi could then direct the invasion of Cambodia, break the will of the Khmer Rouge, and install a pro-Vietnamese regime.

The Chinese accused Vietnam of creating the KNUFNS to support Vietnam's military offensive against Cambodia in order to "realize their long-cherished dream of regional hegemony."[50] Members of China's diplomatic corps began to comment that China might have to attack Vietnam because of provocations along the PRC-SRV border and general instability in Indochina.[51] Thus the situation was ripe for a Chinese-Vietnamese confrontation on two fronts—by proxy along the Vietnam-Cambodian frontier with

Cambodia, and through direct battle along the Sino-Vietnamese border.

In mid-December, the United States and China removed perhaps the last impediment to an all-out invasion of Cambodia by Vietnam. The United States primarily viewed the December 15, 1978 announcement of renewed U.S.-China ties as a natural result of years of negotiation and diplomatic softening between Washington and Beijing. Indeed, the joint communiqué issued by the leaders of both capitals at the time of the announcement made no mention of military cooperation between the two nations. The communiqué did, however, state that both the United States and China were "opposed to efforts by any other country or group of countries to establish . . . hegemony" in the Asia-Pacific region.[52] When asked whether or not the establishment of official relations would worsen China's relations with Russia, Chairman Hua Guofeng stated that the ties affected the United States and China and were not directed against any country. But Chairman Hua then proceeded to mention that American-Chinese ties were favorable to the struggle against hegemonism:

> We have mentioned our opposition to hegemonism in our joint communiqué. We oppose both big hegemony and small hegemony, both global hegemony and regional hegemony. This [the communiqué] will be conducive to the peace of the whole world.[53]

Thus the normalization of U.S.-China relations and the Soviet-Vietnam treaty had a polarizing effect in the Sino-Vietnamese conflict. A SRV embassy official speaking to diplomats in France expressed concern that although U.S.-PRC ties did not surprise Vietnam, Hanoi was nevertheless worried that the diplomatic rapprochement would reinforce the PRC's intention to establish hegemony over Southeast Asia.[54] Vietnam believed that China could now proceed to attack Vietnam and reinforce the military potential of Vietnam's adversary in Cambodia, as the new relationship gave China confidence to stand up to Vietnam and the Soviets.[55]

An Indochina War on Two Fronts

On Christmas Day 1978, Vietnam invaded Cambodia. It was the largest incursion into Cambodia by the Vietnamese in the history of the two countries. Vietnam's intent was to strike a quick fatal blow to the Khmer Rouge leadership in Cambodia and take Phnom Penh in a matter of a week or two, and place their man, Heng Samrin, at the head of the puppet government. The invasion sent shock waves throughout Asia. ASEAN called for an immediate withdrawal, as did the United Nations. Though meeting unexpected resistance, the Vietnamese still found it relatively easy to gain ground against the weaker Cambodian forces.

On January 7, 1979, the People's Republic of Kampuchea was declared, with Heng Samrin as head of state. Despite having captured most urban areas, including Phnom Penh, the Vietnamese military found that resistance in the hill areas of Cambodia was quite strong. The Khmer Rouge retreated to the highlands where it was able to regroup and forestall the Vietnamese drive.

The Chinese foreign ministry issued a statement on January 14, 1979, condemning the attack as "Vietnamese hegemonism abetted by Soviet social-imperialism."[56] Despite calling for international support in condemning the Vietnamese invasion, the statement made no mention of an impending Chinese military reaction against Hanoi. Before and after the Vietnamese attack on Cambodia various Chinese leaders had been quoted as saying that China was probably going to have to "teach Vietnam a lesson."

In early February it became evident that Vietnam's presence in Cambodia was not a temporary one. China's warnings to Vietnam continued. In commenting about China's threats, Vietnamese foreign ministry official Nguyen Duy Trinh stated that Vietnam was ready to talk with China about a cessation of hostilities, working toward a settlement on border/territorial issues, and about the ethnic Chinese issue.[57] Noticeably absent from his remarks was any mention of the Cambodian crisis which constituted the main obstacle dividing China and Vietnam.

The Chinese invasion of Vietnam occurred on February 14,

1979. This was fifteen weeks after the signing of the Vietnamese-Soviet Treaty of Cooperation and Friendship and just six weeks after the Vietnamese invasion of Cambodia. China justified the invasion by referring to the need to counterattack Vietnamese troops which had repeatedly crossed over into Chinese territory and provoked those living along border areas:

> After counterattacking the Vietnamese aggressors as they deserve, the Chinese frontier troops will strictly keep to defending the border of their own country . . . .
> . . . the two sides (should then) speedily hold negotiations at any mutually agreed place "to discuss" the restoration of peace and tranquility along the border.[58]

Official Chinese statements announcing the invasion mentioned only the border incursions as reasons for attack. In addition, China preferred to downplay its invasion at the United Nations, instead bringing attention to Vietnam's invasion of Cambodia.[59]

The Soviet reaction to the invasion of Vietnam was somewhat subdued. Although the official Soviet press agency called the Chinese aggressive and hegemonistic for their incursion into Vietnam, it made it clear that the Soviet response was primarily supportive in nature:

> The heroic Vietnamese people, which has become victim of a fresh aggression, is capable of standing up for itself this time again, and furthermore it has reliable friends. The Soviet Union will honor its obligations under the Treaty of Friendship and Cooperation between the USSR and the Socialist Republic of Vietnam.
> Those who decide policy in Peking should stop before it is too late. . . . All responsibility for the consequences of continuing the aggression by Peking against the Socialist Republic of Vietnam will be borne by the present leadership.[60]

Though the warning from Moscow was firm, there were still indications that the Soviets were not anxious to become involved in the conflict. Most outside observers believed that the Soviet response reflected more of Moscow's desire to portray the PRC as an invader, and to attempt to make the Chinese believe the Soviets would assist Vietnam, though there was no mention as to what kind of help this would involve.[61]

On February 24, the Soviet military attaché to the Soviet embassy in Hanoi reiterated Moscow's warning to the Chinese, but once again stated that the Vietnamese people were capable of defending themselves.[62] The Soviet warnings in both cases came after the Chinese had made public that their intentions were limited in the invasion. Indeed, there was a willingness on the part of the Soviets to assist the Vietnamese with supplies and perhaps intelligence, but the actual fighting was totally left to the Vietnamese so not to bring Soviet troops into direct conflict with the Chinese.[63]

Chinese forces moved six miles into Vietnamese territory within four days, fifteen miles within six days, and finally twenty-five miles deep within nine days (see map 1). But the invasion was costly to China. It was only two weeks into the war before China was suggesting a truce in the fighting and a general cessation of hostilities. Outside observers wondered about China's abilities to deliver matériel into the war zone. In addition, casualties on both sides of the border were mounting, indicating that China was paying dearly for the invasion.[64]

Vietnam agreed peace talks were necessary, but made them contingent on a withdrawal of Chinese forces from Vietnam. It became increasingly clear as the war continued that China's reasons for invading Vietnam were deep-seated, not just in response to border incursions, as Beijing had originally claimed. Deng Xiaoping reiterated that China did not want a single inch of Vietnamese soil, but added China

> cannot tolerate the Cubans to go swashbuckling unchecked in Africa, the Middle East and other areas, nor can we tolerate the Cubans of the Orient to go swashbuckling unchecked in Laos, Cambodia or even China's border area.[65]

Map 1. China's Invasion of Vietnam

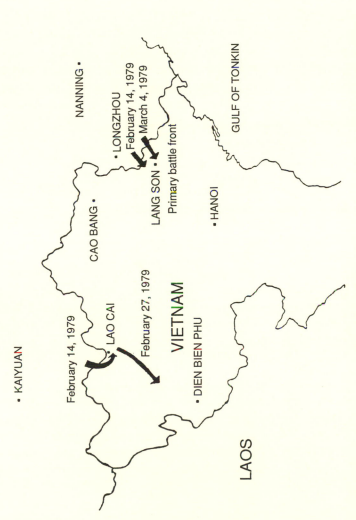

Sources: Office of the Geographer, Bureau of Intelligence and Research, U.S. Department of State, *International Boundary Study No. 38; China-Vietnam Boundary,* December 15, 1978; National Geographic Society, *Asia,* map 02812, 1978.

Despite Deng's statement declaring Vietnam's invasion of Cambodia as a reason for China's attack on Vietnam, the Chinese press continued to send contradictory signals. The Chinese news agency denied that Vietnam's incursion into Cambodia had anything to do with their attack on Vietnam and decidedly held on to the border clashes as reason for China "teaching Vietnam a lesson."

On March 4, China announced it had captured the town of Long Son, and subsequently claimed victory (as did Vietnam) and suggested a pull out was imminent. The following day China announced a formal troop withdrawal.

> The Chinese frontier troops have attained the goals set for them since they were compelled to launch a counterattack in self-defense on February 17 against ceaseless armed provocations and incursions of the Vietnamese aggressors against China.
>
> The Chinese government announces that starting from March 5, 1979, all Chinese frontier troops are withdrawing to Chinese territory.
>
> We do not want a single inch of Vietnamese territory, but neither will we tolerate incursions into Chinese territory. All we want is a peaceful and stable border. We hope that this stand of the Chinese government will be respected by the government of Vietnam and the governments of other countries of the world.
>
> . . . The Chinese government proposes again that the Chinese and Vietnamese sides speedily hold negotiations to discuss ways of insuring peace and tranquility along the border between the two countries and then proceed to settle the boundary and territorial dispute.
>
> . . . At the same time, we hope that all countries . . . will take measures to urge the Vietnamese authorities to stop promptly their aggression against Kampuchea and withdraw all their forces of invasion back to their own territory so as to secure the interest of peace, security and stability of Southeast Asia and of Asia as a whole.[66]

As the announcement suggests, China held deeper concerns in its conflict with Vietnam than simply anger stemming from armed provocations along its border with its southern neighbor. The message was directed to the Soviet Union as well as Vietnam in an attempt to reflect the tough line Beijing was willing to hold in Asia. At the same time, it served to establish the boundaries of its commitment so as not to risk bringing the Soviets into direct involvement in the war.

Radio Hanoi immediately responded to the troop withdrawal announcement and issued the following statement:

> If China really withdraws all of its troops from Vietnam as it has stated, and after all the Chinese forces have been withdrawn to the other side of the historical border that both sides have agreed to respect, then the Vietnamese side will be ready immediately to enter into negotiations with the Chinese side at the deputy foreign ministers' level at a place and date to be agreed upon on the restoration of normal relations.[67]

It is evident that both sides were willing to end the hostilities and were relieved that the war was winding down. The price of the war had been higher than expected for the Chinese, as the Vietnamese were able to muster more resistance than Beijing had originally expected. The Chinese continued to destroy Vietnamese infrastructure as they retreated, actions that prompted a harsh response from Hanoi, though the actions did not jeopardize the prospects for peace talks between the two capitals. By the end of March, reports told the extent of the destruction wrought by the war. Journalist Jean Thoraval reported that 80 percent of the infrastructure in areas where the Chinese invaded was destroyed. Cities were reduced to rubble and mass graves were everywhere.[68]

With the troop withdrawal nearing its end, the Chinese were decidedly more up-front about their reasons for invading Vietnam. On March 18, Beijing listed five reasons for the Chinese need to teach Vietnam a lesson. These included:

1. Vietnam had become a hegemonist power presenting the image of the world's third military superpower.

2. Refusal on the part of Hanoi to recognize the importance of China's borders and the subsequent incursions into Chinese territory.

3. The mistreatment of ethnic Chinese living on Vietnamese soil and their systematic expulsion by the Vietnamese authorities.

4. The oppression of the Vietnamese people through harsh domestic control and through foreign war.

5. The Soviet Union's continued interest in expanding its interests into Southeast Asia in an attempt to mousetrap China by extending the Soviet sphere of influence.[69]

Though the all-out war between China and Vietnam was over, it by no means meant an end to deep hostilities. Border fighting continued and China started rumors of a "second lesson." But for the most part, both Vietnam and China took their differences to the bargaining table and sought immediate ways to prevent a second costly war from occurring. Before turning to an analysis of these efforts in the next chapter, a summary and conclusion is helpful to outline the major issues covered in this chapter.

Conclusion

This chapter makes several propositions about the Vietnam-China relationship from 1975 to 1979. The first proposition is that China and Vietnam differed in their views of what Hanoi's political role should be in Indochina. China feared that a united Vietnam would lead the Vietnamese into seeking a Hanoi-dominated Indochina federation. Hanoi believed that China preferred a divided Vietnam and would try to influence Laos and Cambodia in directions that would not coincide with Vietnam's interests.

The second proposition is that China and Vietnam did not want a total break of relations that would encourage further Soviet involvement in Vietnam's affairs. For this purpose Hanoi sought aid not only from Moscow, but from Beijing as well. Beijing was reluctant to give aid due to what Beijing saw as Hanoi's apparent willingness to seek out Soviet aid and cooperate with Moscow. The rejection of aid led Vietnam closer into the arms of Moscow, which in turn further alienated Beijing.

The third proposition suggests issues that divided China and Vietnam, like the border/territorial conflict and the rift over ethnic Chinese living in Vietnam, were conflicts generated by an overall disagreement between the two countries over the fate of

Indochina. As competing policies clashed over Cambodia, Hanoi and Beijing stepped up their war of words over peripheral conflicts not directly involving the Cambodian crisis.

In addition to these propositions, there are several conclusions that can be drawn from the foregoing discussion:

1. China's and Vietnam's differences reflect security and power considerations that affect all nation-states regardless of ideology. Marxist ideology from 1975 to the conclusion of the 1979 war had little to do with the issues dividing Vietnam and China. Just as East European countries have differed with Moscow in their outlook concerning regional and international relations, the Sino-Vietnamese conflict is principally a traditional example of how nation-states seek to enhance their power vis-à-vis other nation-states.

2. Though China and Vietnam have historically been at odds with one another, the conflict perhaps reflects more of China's and Vietnam's attempts to be recognized as sovereign powers seeking individual national interests, and is less a reflection of nation-states divided by specific cultural/historical differences. There is no doubt history plays an important role in the conflict, but realpolitik considerations are paramount to both Beijing and Hanoi.

3. The conflict also indicates that nation-states opening to the outside world for the first time are anxious to ensure their success as sovereign powers by seeking to increase their influence in regional and international affairs. The period 1975 to 1979 was a period of transition in the domestic and foreign policy arenas for both Vietnam and China. China was anxious to halt the threat of encirclement on its borders to prove its abilities as a regional and world power. Vietnam's reunification gave Hanoi confidence to seek wide recognition in the international community. Hanoi felt, therefore, that pressing for greater influence in Indochina was a logical outgrowth of this newly found confidence.

Though some of the peripheral issues of the Sino-Vietnamese conflict have diminished somewhat in the importance since 1979, the Cambodian conflict remains the principal factor dividing China and Vietnam. The next two chapters look more closely at this aspect of the conflict.

3

Cambodia: A Seemingly Endless Struggle

The Vietnamese invasion of Cambodia and China's subsequent invasion of Vietnam had an impact on the Sino-Vietnamese conflict in terms other than those typically associated with the horrors of war. For the first time since the serious signs of split began to emerge in the mid-1970s, Hanoi and Beijing focused more of their attention on conflicting policies in Indochina, particularly Cambodia, and less on border, territorial, and ethnic problems. Though the two invasions failed to solve any of the problems dividing the two nations, war expressed the degree to which Hanoi and Beijing were willing to advance their aims in Indochina.

This chapter looks at Sino-Vietnamese relations, in particular the continuing struggle for dominance in Indochina, from the close of the 1979 war to late 1986. The first section considers how the war had affected Beijing and Hanoi's view of the situation in Indochina and relations toward each other generally. The second section outlines the strategies the Chinese and Vietnamese have employed in an attempt to gain the upper hand in the conflict. The third section looks at trends indicating a change was forthcoming in the way the two countries dealt with one another. A summary follows.

In War's Aftermath:
The Two Sides State Their Case

Vietnam's invasion of Cambodia had a dramatic effect on the balance of power in Indochina. This was evident to the Chinese who sought to punish Vietnam by launching an invasion of their own. Though the balance of power shifted somewhat in Hanoi's favor in the region following the SRV invasion, the issues at stake remained the same. Vietnam still wanted an Indochinese federation, and China wanted an independent, if not Chinese-dominated, Indochina.

Vietnam's efforts in Cambodia met a serious obstacle. Although Hanoi was able to "liberate" Phnom Penh, the Khmer Rouge were able to retreat to the highlands of Cambodia (along with other resistance groups) and put together an effective defensive strategy to hold the Vietnamese at bay. In addition to receiving aid from the Chinese, the Khmer Rouge proved themselves able to fight a protracted guerrilla war, frustrating Vietnamese efforts to bring all of Cambodia under the control of their puppet leader Heng Samrin.

China's invasion of Vietnam also fell short of its intended results. Chinese leaders were in disagreement as to whether or not China's invasion had actually "taught" Vietnam a lesson. The Chinese were unable to get needed troops and matériel to the battlefront and met unexpected resistance from Vietnamese militia troops, soldiers who were considered poorer fighters than the Vietnamese regulars.[1] Both sides had considerable losses in human life, though Vietnam perhaps "lost" the war in terms of sustaining massive property damage.

Also disappointing to the Chinese was the fact that the invasion had failed to reverse Vietnam's efforts in Cambodia. The invasion did substantially challenge the Vietnamese military forces who were forced to fight on two fronts, but, for the most part, Cambodia was brought under widespread control of the Vietnamese. There is indication that Deng Xiaoping believed that the main purpose of the invasion was to convince the Vietnamese that China's word counted in Indochina.[2] To this end the Vietnamese took note.

The close of the war did not bring about a cessation of open hostilities. Border skirmishes and long-range shelling continued on a regular basis. But the war did slowly bring the two sides closer to the real issues which divided them. Beijing brought the border dispute into focus with its view of Vietnam as a regional hegemonist:

> The facts in the last few years show that Hanoi's armed provocations along the Sino-Vietnamese border are a logical development of its quest for regional hegemony and constituted a link in the Kremlin's strategic dispositions for world hegemony.[3]

The Chinese argued these hegemonistic tendencies could be proven by looking at Vietnam's deeds in the region:

1. The leaders of the SRV have declared Vietnam to be the third military power in the world. This, Beijing contends, proves Vietnam is expansionist in nature.

2. Vietnam has taken territories belonging to China and has invaded its neighbors, making Vietnam a pawn in the USSR's hegemonist approach.

3. The Vietnamese have used external disturbances to keep Vietnam's citizens in line. If Vietnam was satisfactorily meeting its people's needs, there would be less pressure to invade its neighbors.[4]

The Vietnamese contended that since the mid-1970s China had tried to get Vietnam to give up its independence and sovereignty by aligning with Beijing. When this failed, Vice Foreign Minister Phan Hien said China moved into action by:

1. Intruding onto Vietnam's territory without considering the validity of the Franco-Chinese treaty of 1887.

2. Inducing ethnic Chinese residents in Vietnam to provoke riots against the SRV government.

3. Canceling all aid projects and recalling technical specialists. Then Beijing tried to talk other countries out of sending aid to Vietnam.

4. China sought to drive a wedge between Vietnam and other Indochinese countries, and, all in all, encircle Vietnam and bring it into China's orbit.[5]

The two viewpoints expressed above bring to light the fact that both Hanoi and Beijing were at odds with each other principally because they were competing for influence in the region and feared what would happen if the other succeeded. Thus, for the Chinese, border problems, ethnic Chinese problems, and other problems could not be separated from Vietnam's overall ambitions in Indochina because they reflected Hanoi's expansionist tendencies. Similarly, Hanoi believed the border problem, the ethnic Chinese problem, and the other issues at stake resulted from Chinese efforts to contain the Vietnamese and keep Hanoi from spoiling China's intentions in the region.

On April 18, 1979, China and Vietnam began peace talks in Hanoi. For the Chinese, the negotiations centered on the situation in Cambodia. Beijing determined this was the major cause of hostility between China and Vietnam and therefore must be the first issue on the agenda. Vietnam, on the other hand, said that Cambodia had nothing to do with the issues at hand, and that the real issues at stake involved Vietnam and China and not a third party. Hanoi's original three proposals, in fact, only dealt with peripheral issues dividing China and Vietnam:

1. Establish a demilitarized zone along the Sino-Vietnamese border and cease all hostilities toward one another.

2. Restore normal relations between the two countries.

3. Settle the border and territorial conflict as determined by history and agreed upon by the central committees of the two countries.[6]

Though Hanoi admitted that Sino-Vietnamese relations were strained because of competing policies in Indochina, there was no doubt that Vietnam wanted to avoid allowing Cambodia to be an issue considered at the talks. Such a topic of discussion could undermine Vietnam's efforts in Cambodia and, like Geneva in 1954 and Paris in 1973, would signal yet another defeat for the Vietnamese at the bargaining table. Cambodia had become the main foreign policy thrust for Vietnam since 1975 and Hanoi was not about to let the Chinese take control of the issue. Hanoi, therefore, attempted to discuss other issues, hoping that time would allow the Vietnamese military to subdue completely the Khmer Rouge in the highlands of Cambodia.

The Chinese capitalized on this point during the second round of talks on April 26. Han Nianlong accused the Vietnamese of sidestepping the crucial issues that divided the two nations. At the same time, Han presented China's eight principles for improving relations between China and Vietnam, the second principle being the focal point of the document:

> Neither side should seek hegemony in Indochina, Southeast Asia or any other part of the world, and each is opposed to efforts by any other country or group of countries to establish such hegemony.
> Neither side shall station troops in other countries, and those already stationed abroad must be withdrawn to their own country. Neither side shall join any military blocs directed against the other, provide military bases to other countries, or use the territory and bases of other countries to threaten, subvert or commit armed aggression against the other side or against any other countries.[7]

It was clear that agreement on substantial issues was not forthcoming. The Vietnamese continued their insistence that Cambodia was not to be a bargaining chip in the talks. For the Chinese, the Cambodian question was the only point from which meaningful talks could begin. Emphasizing this principle, Han Nianlong, in a somewhat contradictory statement in early May, stated that China "had no preconditions for normalizing relations with the SRV," but Vietnam

> must in the first place put an end to the aggression against Cambodia and withdraw its troops, that Laos must no longer be under total Vietnamese control and they must not continue with their anti-Chinese policy. Otherwise, how can we hope to improve relations?[8]

In the first session of the second round of Sino-Vietnamese talks on June 28, 1979, both sides restated their original proposals. Vietnam was seeking a victory over the Khmer Rouge before bringing up the issue of Cambodia, and China continued to demand a withdrawal of Vietnamese troops before making any new proposals.[9] Amid the new war of words, China fueled talk of a "second punitive lesson" for Vietnam, if the Vietnamese did not begin to make progress on the issues at hand.[10]

Though these disagreements persisted, a dialogue began anew by use of official propaganda. In October, Hanoi issued its white book on Sino-Vietnamese relations. The book was entitled "The Truth About Vietnam-China Relations Over the Last 30 Years."[11] The document detailed what Hanoi saw as a continuation of Chinese deceptions and "sell-outs" of Vietnam since the founding of the People's Republic of China. The main tenets of the white book are summarized below:

1. China is colluding with the United States to oppose liberation movements in Southeast Asia and in particular in Indochina. This is evident from China's moves to establish contact with the United States during Vietnam's struggle against the U.S. imperialists (referring to Nixon and the Shanghai communiqué).

2. Though the Soviet Union is China's chief enemy in Asia, Beijing regards Vietnam as "an important opponent to be subdued and conquered so that its strategic interests are secured."

3. China not only wants to control Vietnam, but all of Southeast Asia. China has tried to keep Vietnam a divided nation on several occasions, beginning with the Geneva talks in 1954, the Paris talks in 1973, and particularly since the occasion of Hanoi's liberating the South in 1975. This was part of an overall strategy by the Chinese to reduce Vietnam's influence over its neighbors, while Beijing used overseas Chinese to control insurgency movements.

4. The Chinese have consistently fostered anti-Vietnamese strategies, evidenced in their trying to prolong the Vietnamese struggle against U.S. imperialism, by seeking to force Vietnam into using Chinese strategies of warfare rather than time-tested Vietnamese strategies.

5. China used Cambodia as a springboard for invading Viet-

nam. China colluded with Pol Pot's regime in order to drive a wedge between Cambodia and Vietnam.

The release of the white book was used to lend legitimacy to Vietnam's role in Cambodia, and to try to put Beijing on the defensive. By late 1979 China had managed to mount support in its condemnation of Vietnam from the United States, the United Nations, ASEAN, and other influential actors in the international community. The Vietnamese desperately needed to gain back some prestige, particularly in view of its unpopular war against the Khmer Rouge. The Chinese, in fact, accused the Vietnamese of issuing the white book in order to gain domestic support from the Vietnamese people, and to escape the international pressures bearing on Vietnam as a result of its aggression in Cambodia.[12]

The Chinese denied all allegations made in Hanoi's white book adding that the drastic worsening in Sino-Vietnamese relations was the result of Vietnam's hegemonist intentions against China and Indochina since 1975.[13] Special emphasis was given to the Vietnamese invasion of Cambodia as a "crucial factor" for deteriorating Sino-Vietnamese relations.

As the war of words continued, the battle for Cambodia proceeded also. The Chinese continued to give arms to the Khmer Rouge. The PLA increased its artillery attacks into Vietnamese territory during the winter dry season in order to burden further Vietnamese efforts in Cambodia. The Chinese hoped that continued military pressure on Vietnam, plus a resistant struggle from the KR, would bring new pressure on Vietnam to reconsider its presence in Cambodia.

Though the Vietnamese were able in the winter of 1980 to take ground held by the KR, they were still not able to bring about total defeat of the guerrilla fighters before the rainy season began. This meant the Chinese had a small victory under their belt in slowing down the Vietnamese military machine. But as the Sino-Vietnamese talks resumed, the issues remained the same and the two sides found themselves as far away from settlement as they had been the previous year. China continued to call for a withdrawal of Vietnamese troops from Cambodia, and Vietnam remained firm in its refusal to bring the Cambodian situation into the Sino-Vietnamese talks. Emphasizing the continuity of this policy, Foreign Minister Nguyen Co Thach told reporters Vietnam would remain in Cambodia and Laos as long as there was a Chinese threat. He stated that he wanted ASEAN and China to understand that a Vietnam-influenced Indochina was a fact.[14]

Unable to break the stalemate in Cambodia, both sides continued their propaganda campaign. The two countries issued documents justifying their claims to disputed territories, condemning the other for its historic stand on ethnic Chinese living in Vietnam, and Hanoi even published a history of where the Chinese revolution went wrong and how the PRC and SRV revolutionary experiences differed.[15] But the underlying conditions for continuing with talks remained unchanged.

The Vietnamese believed that time was on their side. As long as they could maintain the offensive in Cambodia, they hoped ASEAN and China would ease somewhat in their condemnation and realize that a Vietnam-influenced Cambodia was inevitable. Vietnam accused China on many occasions of using its influence in the international community to fuel an anti-Vietnam campaign. China believed that continued international pressure was a key for breaking Vietnam's will to continue in Cambodia. For this reason China repeatedly called for a Vietnamese withdrawal from Cambodia in the United Nations and tried to convince ASEAN that continued pressure on the SRV was the only suitable policy to follow.[16]

As the dry-season fighting began once again during the winter of 1980–81, the SRV was able to increase the territory under its control, but the KR continued to maintain a foothold in the highlands. The apparent stalemate meant that new efforts had to be made by both the SRV and the PRC in the region to break the standoff. Hanoi and Beijing turned to other states to win support for their policies. This was not easy, especially for the Vietnamese who were losing political and financial support.

In April 1980, Denmark pulled out its advisors from Vietnam and refused to offer additional aid. The Soviets too were growing tired of poor economic planning and corruption in the Vietnamese system that was sapping money intended for construction projects. Moscow pushed for a reorganization of the Vietnamese economy more along Soviet lines and encouraged the dismissal of older economic planners in order to ensure consistency in planning. Though several of the Soviet suggestions were heeded, the SRV reacted coolly to Moscow's demands.[17]

In October, the Soviets made yet another proposal to the Vietnamese. They offered to step in and take over direct management of the economic and social organizations of Cambodia so the SRV military could concentrate on rooting out the Khmer Rouge remnants. The Soviets pointed to poor administration, bad bureaucratic attitudes, general inefficiency, and corruption as factors leading to Vietnamese problems in Cambodia. The Vietnamese rejected the Soviet offer and continued to demonstrate their resolve to carry out their Cambodian policies without outside intervention.[18] The Vietnamese ability to turn down the Soviets indicates that the SRV was not under total Soviet power and was independent enough to reject growing Soviet interest in the region. But Hanoi's need for help caused them to look elsewhere for political and economic relief.

Hanoi and Beijing Seek Outside Support

From the beginning of the peace talks in April 1979, the conditions for direct negotiations on settling the Sino-Vietnamese conflict remained the same. The PRC continued to call for a Vietnamese withdrawal from Cambodia and used border violence on many occasions to emphasize this demand. The Vietnamese refused to talk to Beijing about resolving issues until Beijing acknowledged the "realities of the Kampuchean regime in Phnom Penh." While the demands remained unchanged, the tactics both countries used changed somewhat. Both Hanoi and Beijing sought support from neighboring states and international actors to back their individual policies in hope of convincing the other.

This type of strategy was used before 1981, but its importance increased as China and Vietnam realized that a military solution to the Cambodian situation was slow in coming. What follows is a discussion of how the Chinese and the Vietnamese approached other states who shared an interest in the dispute.

ASEAN

Member countries of the Association of Southeast Asian Nations were suspicious of both Chinese and Vietnamese intentions in the region. By late 1980, ASEAN decided that China was less expansionist than Vietnam, and seemed to echo most of Beijing's sentiments toward the Vietnamese presence in Cambodia.[19] For this reason, Beijing sought ASEAN's support in opposing Vietnam's proposals for settling the Cambodian crisis.

ASEAN had refused to acknowledge the Phnom Penh regime since the Vietnamese installed the government in 1979. The organization pledged only to discuss the Cambodian crisis with leaders of the Coalition Government of Democratic Kampuchea (CGDK). These included Khieu Samphan, leader of the Khmer Rouge, Son Sann, leader of the Khmer People's National Liberation Front (a small Cambodian resistance group), and Prince Sihanouk. The reason was not that ASEAN was particularly fond of any of the above leaders, but it is consistent in its call for a UN-supervised election in Cambodia, to allow the people of that country to determine their own fate. ASEAN viewed the Vietnamese invasion of Cambodia as a violation of these ideals.

China has provided ASEAN with real concerns. Some of ASEAN's members view China as a threat to Indochina in the event that the Vietnamese leave. This conclusion is drawn from China's willingness in the past to give support to the Khmer Rouge leader Pol Pot, despite Pot's murderous record while leader of Cambodia. Beijing has been sensitized to this accusation and promised ASEAN that China wished only to have an independent Cambodia based on the self-determination of the Cambodian people.[20]

Thus the strategies for China and Vietnam vis-à-vis ASEAN became clear after the Sino-Vietnamese war of 1979. China sought ways to ensure that ASEAN's goals reflected Beijing's, so to keep regional pressure against Vietnam. Hanoi knew that a united ASEAN would mean further condemnation of Vietnam in Cambodia, therefore the Vietnamese tried to divide ASEAN over the Cambodian crisis.

On a regular basis, Hanoi officials visited the ASEAN states trying to plead Vietnam's case. Through such meetings the SRV attempted to exploit tensions between ASEAN members, in hopes that its united stand against Vietnam would weaken. They also wanted to convince area nations to accept the status quo in Cambodia. If successful, this strategy would undercut China's diplomatic efforts among ASEAN states and strike a severe blow to Chinese desires to drive the Vietnamese out of Cambodia.[21]

Hanoi also told ASEAN members that Cambodia's status was not negotiable and that all three Indochinese states made up a single entity that could not be distinguished. If ASEAN wanted to have negotiations, therefore, these talks had to include all members of the Indochinese federation, and not include China. Hanoi's efforts here were once again designed to minimize Beijing's role in Indochina's future.[22]

China was able to turn ASEAN away from considering any of Hanoi's proposals. This was done in two ways. First, any time it appeared that ASEAN was warming to Vietnamese calls for settling the Cambodian crisis, China stepped up aid to the Khmer Rouge and increased shelling along the Sino-Vietnamese border. In most cases, instances of shelling along the border areas of China and Vietnam coincided with new attempts by either the Vietnamese or Chinese to exert greater influence on issues surrounding the Cambodian situation.[23] China also used the official forum of the United Nations to condemn Vietnam and proclaim China's desire for an independent Cambodia—a move which, to an extent, reassured ASEAN members.[24]

In recent years, China and Vietnam have continued their

ASEAN policies. From time to time, as ASEAN has hinted that it might move closer to one side or the other, flare-ups have occurred, either in the Cambodian highlands or along the Sino-Vietnamese border. This has meant that ASEAN has remained determined to seek a Vietnamese withdrawal before beginning serious talks about Cambodia's future.

The CGDK

In order to combine the resistance efforts of the various Cambodian groups fighting against the Vietnamese, China and ASEAN helped put together the Coalition Government of Democratic Kampuchea (CGDK). The CGDK is comprised of elements including the Khmer Rouge, the Kampuchean People's National Liberation Front, and loyalists to Prince Norodom Sihanouk. The CGDK is a curious united front because its three-part membership is comprised of groups who have fought and on occasion still fight each other bitterly.

In 1981 the CGDK received over 250 tons of arms from the PRC. It was hoped that coalition forces armed with Chinese weapons would bring Vietnam closer to meeting Beijing's and ASEAN's demands.[25] Though they have been effective in waging a war of resistance against the Vietnamese, they have not been successful in gaining territory. Rumors spread that the various groups were in fact fighting among themselves, rather than countering Vietnamese advances. The Chinese made several attempts to patch up the coalition by pledging further Chinese support.[26]

In early 1984 Sihanouk and Son Sann's group joined together to try to oppose the Khmer Rouge. The initial effort failed, however, as both groups realized that although the KR was weak organizationally, it did have the superior military machine and could therefore offer the most resistance to the Vietnamese.[27] Thus the coalition has remained weak and disjointed and ASEAN and China have preferred to work with individual members rather than with the coalition as a group.

The Soviet Union

Regional actors, particularly the ASEAN states, were worried about the prospects of a Soviet-dominated Indochina. While the Soviets were not able to increase their presence significantly in Laos and Cambodia, they were able to secure a firm military presence in Vietnam. By the end of 1980, the Soviets had developed a major naval facility at Cam Ranh bay, complete with a carrier task group, radar installations, command center, and expanded dock facilities. In addition, they had supplied the Vietnamese with over $2 billion worth of military supplies since the 1979 war, which included 330 aircraft, 220 tanks, 242 surface-to-air missiles, 385 artillery pieces, 2 frigates, 4 guided-missile patrol boats, 4 submarine chasers, 2 landing ships, and a minesweeper.[28] Though some of the equipment could be used in Cambodia, a large portion of the aid was probably intended to boost Vietnam's position vis-à-vis China, due to the nature of the supplies (naval vessels, missiles, etc., most of which were of little use against the guerrilla tactics used by the KR in Cambodia). This enabled Vietnam to continue with its efforts in Cambodia, while at the same time providing the SRV military with additional equipment in the event of a second Chinese invasion.[29]

For this reason alone, ASEAN has been far more willing to cooperate with the Chinese over the Cambodian situation than with the Vietnamese, whom they see as working in tandem, to a degree, with the Soviets in the region. The Chinese have tried to keep this fear constantly on the minds of the ASEAN leaders, by repeatedly claiming that the Soviet goals are directly linked with those of Vietnam throughout the Southeast Asian region:

> The general background and underlying cause for the turbulent situation in Indochina and Southeast Asia in recent years and the worsening relations between China and Vietnam is the emergence of Vietnamese regional hegemonism and the Soviet hegemonistic expansion in Southeast Asia.[30]

These charges continued in hopes that ASEAN would remain convinced that the Vietnamese domination of Cambodia was the result of a growing Soviet presence in the Southeast Asian region.[31]

Vietnam, on the other hand, has tried to make it clear that although the Soviets do have advisors in the various Indochinese states, both Hanoi and Moscow are devoted to the principles of self-determination and sovereignty. Thus, the Soviet Union has no hegemonistic demands, Hanoi contends, but is present in countries only when invited by host governments. In recent years, however, Vietnam has made less mention of the Soviet presence in Indochina in its official rhetoric, possibly an indication that ASEAN was not buying the Soviet and Vietnamese attempts to ease fears in the region.[32]

Generally speaking, ASEAN states have believed that the Soviets do pose a threat in the region. This is evidenced by ASEAN's willingness to discuss military affairs with the United States in the region, and in fact to encourage the United States to maintain a strong presence in the region to counter Soviet influence.[33]

The Indochina Federation

Hanoi has repeatedly made demands that any talk of a Vietnamese pull out of the region must be discussed in the company of the other two members of the Indochinese federation, i.e., the Phnom Penh regime, and members of the Laotian government. Until recently both were viewed by Beijing as Vietnamese puppets. (China recently announced it had decided to "restore friendly relations" and exchange ambassadors with Laos.)[34]

The ASEAN states have been more willing to meet with Laotian leaders than the Chinese have been, but at the same time they realize that they are only a third party in the conflict and are not at will to effect any real change in the situation. Overall reaction by the Chinese and ASEAN to Hanoi's talks involving members of the Indochinese federation proposal are predictable, seen only as a continuing public relations effort on the part of the SRV.

The United States

When Ronald Reagan took office in 1981, he repeatedly made a point about the American involvement in wars like the one the United States fought in Indochina. He promised the American people "no more Vietnams." Unfortunately for Vietnam, this translated into an uncompromising attitude toward Vietnam on the refugee crisis and the conflict in Cambodia. Reagan viewed the continuing Cambodian crisis as demonstrative of Vietnamese and Soviet foreign policies in general, and not a particular problem unique to Indochina.

Reagan's dislike for the Vietnamese regime was evident. Talks on American MIAs suffered a serious breakdown in 1983, despite Vietnam's attempts to rekindle talk of normalization and the return of some American MIA remains. The United States finally publicly recognized significant moves the Vietnamese had made on the issue to continue the accounting process in September of that year.[35] But cooperation on the part of the United States was slow in coming. Hanoi disliked many of the U.S. statements concerning Vietnam's lack of humanitarian concern. The Hanoi authorities also said that recovery of MIAs at times was slowed by increased harassment from PRC troops—an apparent effort to get the United States to pressure the PRC into giving in somewhat on its support of the KR.[36]

Reagan took a hard-line stand against China during the early months of his administration in order to appease Taiwan, only to seek improvement later over a variety of issues ranging from trade to selling military hardware in order to beef up Chinese defenses. The resumption of normal Beijing-Washington communication had a chilling effect on Vietnam. The stalemate in the crisis suited Washington to a degree because it allowed the United States to have good relations with Thailand during a time considered strategically crucial by the Reagan administration, and kept up the pace of cooperation between the United States and the PRC.

The United Nations and the International Community

Vietnam has failed miserably in trying to gain a sympathetic ear at the UN and among influential members of the international community. Vietnam's invasion of Cambodia and the subsequent refugee crisis was enough to shift almost permanently world opinion against Vietnam. China and ASEAN worked hand in hand in keeping up the condemnation of Vietnam, which has in part kept the Vietnam-supported regime from gaining UN recognition.[37] Democratic Kampuchea continues to hold Cambodia's UN seat, which has added to Vietnam's woes in the international community.

International pressure on Vietnam has made it difficult for the SRV to secure aid from sources other than the Soviet Union and COMECON members. Furthermore, few countries have been willing to even consider Vietnam's side of the Cambodian situation as indicated by UN voting patterns where condemnation for Vietnamese activities in the region have been overwhelming.[38] As a result, no UN aid has been received in Cambodia since 1978.

Despite this enormous pressure, Vietnam refused to remove troops from Cambodia, indicating it was getting enough assistance from the Soviets to maintain a presence, despite widespread international condemnation.

China's and Vietnam's early attempts to effect change in the Cambodian situation by influencing outside actors failed to change the stalemate. But signs of change did surface, indicating Beijing and Hanoi were growing weary of war.

Changes in the Wind

In the years immediately following the 1979 war, Beijing expressed concern at third parties seeking to have talks with Hanoi, for fear that agreements might be reached that were less than acceptable to China.

By mid-1983, however, Thailand let Vietnam know it was willing to begin talks on security issues along the Thai-Cambodian border—a move it feared might damage relations with the PRC, but felt was necessary to break the stalemate of the Cambodian crisis. Beijing voiced concern over Bangkok's overtures, but the offer for talks did not have any lasting effect on Sino-Thai relations.[39] In addition, China was beginning to view the Soviets in a somewhat more positive light. Beijing acknowledged that there was a distinct difference of opinion on matters involving the SRV and USSR. Trade between China and the Soviet Union began to increase and China said the two nations "agreed to disagree" over the situation in Afghanistan.[40]

In early 1984, Beijing demonstrated that it was willing to compromise somewhat on the issue. Zhao Ziyang stated that although China did not want direct talks with Vietnam on the future of Cambodia until all of Hanoi's troops were withdrawn, China did not object to other countries conducting talks with Hanoi.[41] The statement failed to mark a significant change of posture on the part of the Chinese, but it was nevertheless a signal that China might be more willing to make compromises if it perceived goodwill on the part of the Vietnamese.

These signs, though more symbolic than demonstrating an actual willingness on the part of Beijing to compromise on the Cambodian issue, indicated that the stress of the situation was bearing heavily on both Beijing and Hanoi. In mid-summer 1984, Hanoi and Phnom Penh admitted success against the CGDK resistance was slow in coming and the long war was taking a toll on both SRV and PRK troops.[42] Internal dissent within the armed forces increased as morale suffered, due to unclear military and political objectives. Many troops were forced to retake areas they had "liberated" on several occasions before, only to lose them later to the Khmer resistance fighters armed with Chinese weapons and trained in guerrilla warfare tactics.

In early 1985, Vietnam launched its largest operation into the Cambodian highlands since its 1978–79 invasion, hoping to soften ASEAN toward compromise on Vietnam's presence in

Cambodia. China retaliated against Vietnam by sending weapons to the Khmer resistance, and by shelling Sino-Vietnam border areas. Though the Chinese response was considered credible and still reflected a commitment to the forces of the Khmer Rouge, speculation was emerging that China was leaning toward other avenues in handling the situation.[43] Some observers believed that China was moving closer toward diplomacy with Hanoi. Although Beijing had no intention of compromise on Vietnam's pull out of Cambodia before negotiating on Cambodia's future, total pull out was perhaps not necessary for Beijing and Hanoi to begin talks. This was based on several assumptions:

1. China was seeking better relations with the USSR, as was Moscow with Beijing. The SRV's continued involvement in Cambodia was slowing down progress in this area. The Chinese began pressuring Moscow to encourage Vietnam to pull out of Cambodia so that PRC-USSR ties could improve. This prospect worried Hanoi.

2. The cost in lives, prestige, and money was too great for China to launch a second major invasion of Vietnam. By mid-1985, the support of ASEAN against the Vietnamese was considered superior to the success of military threats. Thus the military option was diminishing as a viable option for Beijing. This meant cooperation from ASEAN and the international community was necessary for China to continue to pressure the Vietnamese.[44]

The coming to power of Mikhail Gorbachev in March 1985 marked the beginning of new progress in Sino-Soviet relations. Gorbachev immediately encouraged the signing of a joint Chinese-Soviet commission to handle economic, technical, trade, and cultural exchanges. Party-to-party relations improved slightly, and the USSR hinted that change might be forthcoming in Indochina.[45] China reciprocated by indicating that the three steps to improving relations between China and the Soviet Union could be altered somewhat. In addition, China began to refer to the USSR as a socialist state instead of a superpower, as it had for several decades.[46]

In hopes that a compromise on the part of the SRV was possible, the CGDK put forward an eight-point proposal in 1986. Its main points included:

1. Hanoi should sit down with the tripartite group, and other countries to discuss the withdrawal of Vietnamese troops from Cambodia.

2. A total withdrawal of troops is not necessary to begin the talks process.

3. After agreement on a withdrawal process, a cease fire will be monitored by UN observers.

4. After the Vietnamese withdrawal begins, Heng Samrin should enter into talks with the CGDK.

5. The CGDK and the Phnom Penh regime will then hold free elections under a UN observer group.

6. Cambodia will be restored as an independent nation, free, democratic, and nonaligned.[47]

Though there was support for the CGDK proposal from Beijing, the PRC stood firm on a SRV withdrawal before China would normalize relations with Vietnam. This did not, however, keep the Chinese from encouraging Vietnam to consider the partial withdrawal and talk process forwarded by the CGDK. The SRV remained hesitant, as did the Phnom Penh regime, over the CGDK proposal and continued to buy time. For Hanoi to accept the CGDK proposal would be an indication that it was tired of the ongoing struggle and would lend legitimacy to the CGDK if it decided to negotiate. It nevertheless was in a difficult position since its armed struggle against the Cambodian resistance was reaping few positive results.

In addition to the CGDK proposal, leadership changes in Vietnam were also fueling talk of a possible breakthrough. Though Vietnam had never particularly cared for any of China's top leaders, it was clear that China preferred Ho Chi Minh to the leadership that took over after Ho's death. China claimed that the Le Duan/Le Duc Tho "clique" took an opposite path than did Ho Chi Minh and that they were "impossible" to work with.[48] This accusation is probably based on the fact that Ho was able to steer a middle ground between Beijing and Moscow, while the party leadership since Ho had gone over to the Soviet camp.

Meanwhile Moscow and Beijing continued the pace of their contacts. In April an agreement was signed to send technicians to China to assist with industrial and technology projects, the first such agreement since Soviet technicians were recalled by Moscow in 1960. The event did not mean the cooperative days of Sino-Soviet relations had returned, but it did mark another significant step in the improvement of Sino-Soviet ties.[49] Moscow's willingness to cooperate with Beijing came despite the USSR's strong commitment to Hanoi. As Moscow saw no acceptable solution to the problem in Cambodia, there was widespread speculation that Moscow was considering options to lessen its support for Vietnam's Cambodian policy.[50]

On July 28, Mikhail Gorbachev delivered a speech in the Pacific port of Vladivostok calling for an increased role in East Asia for the Soviet Union. He indicated that the USSR had been too isolated in Asia, primarily as a result of attention to military power at the expense of enhancing economic possibilities there. The speech reflected the Soviets' desire to break out of their relative isolation and seek ways to develop the Soviet economy and improve relations with Asian states.

Gorbachev's speech emphasized the importance of China, not only as a neighbor to the Soviet Union, but as a socialist state that plays a vital role in international development. He praised the improved state of relations between the two communist giants, and expressed hope that cooperation would lead to more two-way trade, cultural exchanges, technical and scientific assistance, and a settlement of border disputes. Gorbachev also praised ASEAN's efforts in Asia, both politically and economically, and stressed a hope that relations could improve between the Soviets and the ASEAN states.

The most important part of Gorbachev's speech was his stated belief that relations in all of the above-mentioned areas depended on ending the Afghan war and solving the problem in Cambodia. In terms of the later conflict, Gorbachev stated that much depended on the normalization of Chinese-Vietnamese relations, thus minimizing Chinese demands for the Soviets to pressure Vietnam into a withdrawal from Cambodian soil.[51]

Despite placing responsibility for the problem in Cambodia on the shoulders of Hanoi and Beijing, the message was clearly a positive sign for Beijing and the Southeast Asian states, as well as a warning to the Vietnamese to begin rethinking their role in Cambodia. Hanoi's reaction to Gorbachev's speech was cautious. It was clear some leaders agreed that a settlement was needed, not only for the Soviet's benefit, but for Vietnam's benefit as well. The aging Vietnamese hierarchy, however, offered no indications of a reevaluation of their Cambodia policy. By late summer, however, change was in the air.

Le Duan died on July 10, 1986, leaving his post as the VCP secretary to another member of the anti-China faction, Troung Chinh.[52] But by late summer speculation began that Troung Chinh's tenure as party secretary would be short-lived, as Vietnam's "younger" leaders (approximately sixty years of age) were anxious to remove the old guard.[53] Such a purge did occur in December 1986, as Premier Pham Van Dong, Secretary Troung Chinh, and party strategist Le Duc Tho "resigned" because of poor health and advanced age. Nguyen Van Linh, generally thought of as a reformer, replaced Chinh as party chief. The shake-up was the VCP's largest in four decades and indicated that economic policies of liberalization would be forthcoming.[54]

Though the new party leadership was considered more open in its approach to Vietnamese policies, its Cambodia policy did not differ radically from that of its predecessors. The new party leadership renewed its pledge to continue its "special relationship" with Indochina.[55] But in days immediately following the shifts in the VCP, Phnom Penh announced it was willing to talk with Prince Sihanouk—the indicating partial success of the CGDK proposal and movement within Hanoi's new leadership. This followed attempts by Laos to normalize relations with Beijing, and apparent pressure by the Soviets on Hanoi to deal with the Cambodian crisis—a move not reassuring to Hanoi, which knew that the Soviets and the Chinese were discussing Cambodia in their talks.[56]

There were other positive signs in 1986. In early autumn, Vietnam sent trade delegates to Beijing to discuss Vietnamese participation in an international business convention. Negotiations appeared to go well, and the Vietnamese participated in the Beijing exhibition without incident.[57] In mid-1986, Vietnam attended a sporting event in China and indications were good that low-level contacts would continue between the two countries.[58]

During the first few days of January 1987, the worst fighting between China and Vietnam since the 1979 war occurred along the border. Though both sides accused the other of the provocations, it is difficult to read just how serious the clashes were.[59] The fighting may have been a typical Chinese response to the annual dry-season offensive by Vietnam in Cambodia.[60] On the other hand, the clashes may have been a way to test the waters, by either Hanoi or Beijing, after the new VCP leadership change. At any rate, the fighting, which lasted about a week, did not indicate a major shift in objectives for either China or Vietnam.

Conclusion

In the first chapter of this study, it was mentioned that the main source of contention between China and Vietnam was competition for influence in Indochina. It is hoped that the preceding and present chapter have demonstrated the validity of this assumption. Before beginning the next chapter, it is worth summarizing some of the major features of the Sino-Vietnamese conflict:

1. Conflict over the status of Indochina, particularly Cambodia, remained the fundamental cause of the conflict between China and Vietnam. Though this has been repeated on several occasions, it is nevertheless significant because this aspect is the key to understanding other aspects of the Sino-Vietnamese conflict. As Pao-min Chang suggested in 1983:

> Kampuchea is rooted in a fundamental clash between Chinese and Vietnamese perceptions of the status of Kampuchea in Indochina. . . . Beijing could not but consider any attempt at subjugating Kampuchea

as a direct challenge to its own status as a major power and its credibility. . . . Such a challenge becomes all the more intolerable when it comes from Vietnam—a former protegé—backed by an archenemy, the Soviet Union.[61]

Even after the Vietnamese invasion of Cambodia in 1978–79 and the subsequent China-Vietnam war in that same year, China continued to make every effort to reverse the Vietnamese presence in Cambodia through diplomatic, military, and psychological means. As one instrument seemed to weaken, namely the military option, increased attention was paid to ASEAN and the international community.

Vietnam hoped that time would eventually soften, if not China's, at least ASEAN's position, thus increasing the possibilities for a permanent Vietnamese presence in Cambodia. Though lacking the kind of international support the PRC has had, Vietnam has nevertheless been successful in maintaining its presence in Cambodia.

2. The Sino-Vietnamese conflict has tremendous implications for both Beijing and Hanoi in viewing themselves as regional and world powers. For this reason, the stalemate in Cambodia became even more understandable as both feared a loss of not only regional influence should their opponent win the battle for Indochina, but a loss of international prestige as well. Indeed, both China and Vietnam have gone to great lengths in the last decade to increase their international postures. A defeat by one or the other over the issue of Cambodia could bring into question the abilities of an emerging power.

3. Historical, cultural, and ideological factors do not figure as prominently in this conflict as some have suggested. It is true that China and Vietnam have had troubles for over 2,000 years. It is also true that Vietnam and China, like China and the Soviet Union, accuse each other of sidestepping proper Marxist principles of behavior. Although these aspects of the dispute complicate the issues at hand, they do not represent significant factors at present. Similarly, the problems of the ethnic Chinese living in Vietnam and the border/territorial disputes are also peripheral issues that cloud the major point of contention.

4

Diplomacy:
A Break in the Stalemate

The modest changes of 1985 and 1986 led to hopes for a solution to the Cambodian stalemate and a warming of relations between China and Vietnam. Though Beijing maintained a firm stand against Hanoi, it became clear that progress was being made to finally address the situation in Indochina—the major point of contention between China and Vietnam. This chapter looks at the first serious break in the China-Vietnam conflict since the 1979 war.

After examining the talk proposals forwarded by Hanoi and Phnom Penh, Sihanouk met with Phnom Penh's prime minister, Hun Sen, in December 1987. The first two sections of this chapter look at these developments. In the spring of 1988, the SRV announced a troop withdrawal and renewed an offer to participate in informal talks with the various Cambodian factions. The next section is devoted to these proposals within the context of greater involvement from the superpowers in attempting to end the stalemate. The third section covers the diplomatic give-and-take of the "Jakarta Informal Meeting," as it was called, that brought the warring Cambodian factions together for the first time. The last section looks at the Paris peace talks of 1989, Vietnam's withdrawal from Cambodia, and efforts to form an all-Cambodian Supreme National Council. A conclusion follows.

Testing the Waters

Several significant breakthroughs came in 1987. In early spring, Vietnam expressed a desire to reach a negotiated settlement to the Cambodian situation. SRV Foreign Minister Nguyen Co Thach announced that Vietnam was ready to talk to China and the ASEAN nations about ending the war in Cambodia. Soviet Foreign Minister Shevardnadze was present when Thach made the announcement, indicating that the Soviets supported and perhaps initiated the move.[1] The Chinese quickly dismissed the overtures as rhetoric and accused the Vietnamese of sending up a smoke screen. Hanoi's announcement followed Soviet proposals through Moscow's ambassadors in Thailand and Malaysia to create a mechanism for beginning a dialogue on Cambodia which would include the USSR, China, and the United States.[2]

Little notice was given to Vietnam's offer due to what ASEAN, China, and the CGDK perceived as another round of Hanoi's tactics to whitewash the Vietnamese role in Cambodia. In addition, infighting between the three factions of the CGDK prevented Sihanouk and others from carefully considering Hanoi's offer. Sihanouk renewed threats to quit the coalition, citing the lack of cooperation and the Khmer Rouge's hesitation to give Sihanouk the leverage he needed to deal with the various parties wrapped up in the Cambodia quagmire.

In an attempt to break the stalemate, Indonesian Foreign Minister Mochtar Kusumaatmadja arranged a July meeting in Vietnam to discuss the possibility of convening talks among the various Khmer parties. Mochtar and Nguyen Co Thach's six-hour meeting resulted in a "cocktail party" proposal to include all Khmer factions as a first step to address the Cambodia question. The idea was not a new one, but Hanoi's willingness to participate in the "informal meeting" was a change from the previous Vietnamese stand.[3]

The Khmer Rouge and KPNLF resisted the idea, however. The two factions of the CGDK believed that the Phnom Penh regime was willing to meet with Sihanouk, but did not believe that Khmer Rouge and KPNLF interests were taken to be as important as those of the other parties involved. In addition, the ASEAN countries were less than satisfied with the idea once details of the affair revealed that the agenda called for a meeting of rival Khmer factions first, only to be joined by Vietnamese participants later. Thailand considered this to be letting Hanoi off the hook as aggressor in the Cambodian conflict, and subsequently urged Hanoi and Mochtar to reconsider the CGDKs eight-point proposal of March 1986 (see previous chapter).[4]

In early September, Hanoi tried to keep the idea of a conference alive by stating that Vietnam would attend a political conference as a party directly involved in the Cambodian situation, if the Phnom Penh regime was given diplomatic status at the meeting. The suggestion was flatly rejected by ASEAN and China. The Chinese argued that Hanoi's proposals were part of a Vietnamese ploy to trick area nations and give Vietnam an upper hand in negotiations. Beijing reiterated its demand for a complete Vietnamese withdrawal from Cambodia. Talk of a political conference appeared to wither.[5]

Despite this initial failure, PRK Prime Minister Hun Sen kept up the pressure and presented a four-point plan to the CGDK: (1) Prince Sihanouk would hold a high-ranking position in a coalition Cambodian government, (2) the PRK would agree to a SRV withdrawal from Cambodia, (3) fair elections would be set up, and (4) an international conference on Cambodia would be convened to include Western nations.[6] Sihanouk initially rejected the offer as "trickery," as did the Chinese who argued that any talks over Cambodia must be preceded by a military withdrawal of SRV forces.[7] But the Phnom Penh proposal was significant in that it marked the first time the regime had offered to hold elections with foreign observers present, and had agreed to set up a coalition government to rule an independent, nonaligned Cambodia. It also promised a role for all rival Khmer groups, including the Khmer Rouge, if Pol Pot and his associates were denied participation in the coalition government. Though China continued to stress the same Vietnamese withdrawal precondition, Prince Sihanouk showed interest in the offer.[8]

The Hun Sen–Norodom Sihanouk Meetings

As the United Nations issued its ninth resolution calling for a withdrawal of Vietnamese troops from Cambodia, Hanoi once again called for a political settlement to the conflict. Though no details were included in Hanoi's announcement, the Vietnamese move, along with other overtures from Phnom Penh and Moscow, prompted Prince Sihanouk to consider the offer from Hun Sen to meet in France and discuss the Cambodian conflict. Beijing gave only lukewarm endorsement to the idea and reiterated its demands that the key to a Cambodian settlement rested with Hanoi, not Phnom Penh.[9]

Sihanouk's initial reaction at the meeting with Hun Sen in early December was positive. Despite turning down Sen's offer to assume a high-level post in Phnom Penh and pledging to continue the struggle against Vietnamese troops, a joint declaration was issued calling on the Khmer Rouge and the KPNLF to join in the talks process.[10] The most significant outcome of the meeting was the following set of proposals:

1. An agreement to hold elections in Cambodia.
2. A political settlement based on negotiation must be adhered to.
3. An international conference to assure the sovereignty and legitimacy of Cambodia would be convened.
4. The two parties would meet again in January 1988.[11]

Noticeably absent from the declaration was any mention of China and Vietnam. In fact, the Chinese refused direct comment on the talks, a likely indication that they were not enthusiastic about the meeting of Sihanouk and Hun Sen.[12] The Chinese hierarchy was perturbed with Prince Sihanouk's willingness to negotiate a settlement on the issue without pressuring Vietnam to withdraw first. Vietnam, on the other hand, enthusiastically supported the talks. The Soviet Union also showed interest in the talks in order to lessen some of its financial commitment to the expensive Cambodian operation.[13]

Despite Sihanouk's optimistic response to his talks with Hun

Sen, his mood quickly changed. On December 10, Sihanouk announced that he would cancel his January meeting with Hun Sen, citing as the primary reason the Khmer Rouge and KPNLF's unwillingness to join Sen and Sihanouk.[14] In addition, Sihanouk called Hun Sen "Vietnam's valet," adding that future talks should include Hanoi as a full partner in the discussions.[15] He furthermore called on Vietnam to withdraw its forces from Cambodia so that meaningful talks could resume.

Despite obvious speculation that Sihanouk had heard from angry Chinese leaders in the talks' aftermath, Beijing played down its role in the affair. The Chinese foreign ministry stated that China respected Sihanouk's efforts and supported the "unity and cooperation of the ASEAN countries and highly praise their efforts to urge Vietnam to withdraw its troops from Kampuchea so to achieve a political settlement." In an about-face, Sihanouk announced that he was rescheduling his meeting with Hun Sen due to ASEAN pressure. Though China did not block the planned talks, it did accuse Phnom Penh and Hanoi of launching a campaign to split the CGDK, by sowing disunity among the various members of the coalition, seeking international recognition of the Phnom Penh regime, and pressuring Sihanouk to participate in talks without direct Vietnamese representation.[16]

In an attempt to promote unity among the anti-Vietnamese ranks, Sihanouk proposed two conditions going into the talks with Hun Sen: a Vietnamese troop withdrawal and the establishment of a noncommunist government in Phnom Penh.[17] When the talks were convened, both sides were tough in their bargaining positions. Phnom Penh demanded the elimination of the Khmer Rouge from the CGDK coalition, and Sihanouk called for the Vietnamese to present a timetable for withdrawing troops and an agreement to establish a democratic government in Cambodia. While Vietnam publicly announced its willingness to withdraw from Cambodia by 1990 if rival parties could agree on it,[18] Sihanouk acknowledged that it was virtually impossible to eliminate the Khmer Rouge because of its military strength, adding that China and Vietnam needed to reach an agreement on that issue. Sihanouk's statement was indicative of his limited role in seeking a lasting agreement, without the two regional superpowers coming to some sort of agreement between themselves.[19]

To reemphasize China's demands for a Vietnamese troop withdrawal, China shelled the Vietnamese border during the second round of talks. It was the first such attack against the Vietnamese in a year that most observers had proclaimed the most peaceful since fighting between Vietnam and China broke out nine years before. It may have also been Beijing's desire to remind Sihanouk to push for a Vietnamese withdrawal at all costs, though it is doubtful Sihanouk paid much attention to the renewed border flare-up.

The second round of talks ended January 21, 1988, without a major public statement and without agreement on specific demands lodged by either side. The two leaders did agree to meet a third time in North Korea, with subsequent meetings in France and New Delhi. The absence of a Vietnamese commitment to withdraw its troops and Sihanouk's insistence to include all members of the CGDK in any future government coalition in Phnom Penh seemed to be the major stumbling blocks.[20] Despite the apparent impasse, Prince Sihanouk gave a positive report to foreign reporters, stating that there was a 50 percent chance of finding a solution to the situation in Cambodia.[21]

Just two days after the second round of talks ended, Sihanouk announced his resignation, blaming KPNLF leader Son Sann for discrediting his attempts in talks with Hun Sen. At first, Sihanouk's resignation was seen as a hopeful sign for Phnom Penh and Hanoi, both of which considered Sihanouk more willing to accept a compromise than the Chinese and other members of the CGDK.[22] It later became apparent that Sihanouk's strategy was primarily designed to get Beijing to support his efforts in the negotiation process and to lessen China's willingness to stand behind the Khmer Rouge. Sihanouk's strategy worked in part, as Zhao Ziyang announced broad support of Sihanouk's initiative to settle the conflict.[23] In addition, Sihanouk announced that he would cancel his talks with Hun Sen and offered to meet with

Hanoi directly to discuss the problem. As a party not affiliated with the Khmer Rouge, Sihanouk probably felt his chances of meeting with the Hanoi authorities would be enhanced.

Hanoi's initial reaction was one of caution, choosing to study the proposal.[24] Vietnam then rejected the offer, stating that Cambodian parties needed to solve that country's internal problems and then Vietnam would take part in a second round of "cocktail party" talks—thus returning to the Indonesian foreign minister's suggestion of the previous July.

The other members of the CGDK shortly thereafter called on Sihanouk to resume his position as president of the coalition. Sihanouk announced his resolve to work with the Khmer Rouge, but remained firm in his condemnation of the KPNLF.[25] The prince's son assumed charge of Sihanouk's post.

Beijing realized that with Sihanouk holding out, prospects for a settlement were stalled. This meant it had to try to smooth the latest rift in the CGDK. By mid-February, the feuding factions of the coalition were united in their overtures for Sihanouk to resume his role as leader of the CGDK government.[26] The Sihanouk plan worked. Beijing moved to consolidate the other members of the faction, and on the surface at least, the Chinese were forced to pledge their support for Sihanouk's peace initiative.[27] Sihanouk won verbal support from all anti-Vietnamese parties to work for a quadripartite interim government for Cambodia, which would include the CGDK and the Phnom Penh regime until elections could be held. But the sticky issue of a Vietnamese troop withdrawal was not discussed openly.

Signs also surfaced that the Soviets were pushing for Sihanouk to stay on board with discussions. An unnamed Soviet diplomat told the French press agency that Soviet officials would be willing to meet with Sihanouk during the course of the political settlement discussions. The statement was a radical departure from previous statements out of the Soviet Union, where Sihanouk was not recognized as having any relevance to the Cambodian situation.[28] The statement was also perhaps a way of getting the Vietnamese to move closer to direct talks with

Sihanouk. ASEAN diplomats had been noticing for some time a marked change in how the USSR was handling its affairs in Asia, a factor that undoubtedly worried Hanoi.[29]

On March 1, Sihanouk announced he had withdrawn his resignation and was ready to continue searching for a solution to the Cambodia problem. Though there was little doubt that he would in fact retake his post, his timing was perfect, perhaps deliberately so, to resume talks with Hun Sen. Sen told reporters that the prospects for a settlement were good, in which a quadripartite coalition comprised of all the political parties of the CGDK could participate, providing the armies of the KPNLF and Khmer Rouge were disbanded. He set no timetable for a Vietnamese withdrawal, only stating that it was inevitable that all Vietnamese troops would be out by 1990. Hun Sen's remarks confirmed Phnom Penh's understanding that Sihanouk must represent all three members of the CGDK if progress was to be made. It also implied that Vietnam may have agreed to a government with Khmer Rouge elements, providing its participation was non-military in nature.

It is unclear what role the Soviets played in the SRV's willingness to allow a political role for the KR. Moscow had been making attempts to give ASEAN nations a more positive image of the Soviet Union in Asia. Admitting that Vietnam was a "bad example of socialism," Moscow was able to increase its contacts with area leaders. ASEAN responded favorably to the Soviet overtures for two principal reasons. First, most area nations no longer believed the Soviet Union posed a serious military threat to the region. Second, Moscow had become openly critical of Vietnam's mismanagement of aid monies and go-nowhere policies in Cambodia.[30]

In late March, Vietnamese Foreign Minister Thach ruled out a face-to-face meeting with Sihanouk, but agreed that an exchange of letters would be possible. He downplayed the significance of the statement, however, reiterating that Hanoi could play no role in a problem that was ostensibly Cambodian in nature. He did, however, renew his pledge to join in informal talks after Cambodian factions had first met to discuss their problems.[31] Though Thach's statement did not indicate a major policy change, it is significant in comparison to where Vietnam had stood several years earlier, when Hanoi ruled out any discussions that included the Khmer Rouge and omitted China.

A Withdrawal and a "Cocktail" Offer

For two months there was little movement on the diplomatic front. The major reason for this was a shift in the focus of the conflict to the Vietnam-China territorial dispute. China had increased its presence in the South China Sea, in particular around the Spratly Island chain, and Vietnam tried to prevent China from doing so. This led to fierce clashes in March and April amid speculation that the Chinese intended to develop the Spratlys, in order to put further pressure on Vietnam to find a solution in Cambodia (though the Chinese seem to have had the goal of reclaiming the Spratlys for a long time).

By mid-May, movement began anew on the diplomatic front. Prince Sihanouk announced he wanted to continue talking with Hun Sen sometime during the year. He hinted that success along this front might be enhanced if Phnom Penh became more independent of Vietnam. Phnom Penh was conciliatory in its response, suggesting that the main problem in delaying the talk process was the Khmer Rouge and their continued support from China.[32]

At the same time signs emerged that suggested there was hope in solving a major stumbling block. Thai Foreign Minister Siddhi Savetsila reported that Eduard Shevardnadze promised Moscow would talk to Vietnam about ending its occupation of Cambodia.[33] Indeed, there was speculation among many observers, and hope among the Chinese, that the Soviet pull out of Afghanistan would lead to a Vietnamese pull out of Cambodia, clearing the way for the eventual normalization of relations between China and the Soviet Union. On May 26, Hanoi announced that it was pulling out 50,000 troops from Cambodia by the end of the year.

It also said it was willing to participate in the "cocktail party" meeting agreed to earlier and meet with Prince Sihanouk.[34] It was not clear if the Vietnamese intended to meet with all parties involved, or to wait until the second stage as the original agreement stipulated (the first stage was to include Cambodian factions only). Vietnam and the Soviet Union both strongly urged the participation of the Chinese in the cocktail meeting. The request was denied by the Chinese, fearful that involvement in any forum like the cocktail party would drag China into a situation where China might have to share blame and responsibility for the problems in Cambodia.

Phnom Penh agreed to meet with Sihanouk again, though a time was not proposed. China endorsed the talks, calling on Vietnam to commit to a total withdrawal and get directly involved in the talk process.[35] But Vietnam announced that although it was willing to participate in the cocktail party, it would only be at the second stage of the meeting, after the Khmer factions had met, thus maintaining its previous position. A few days later, Hanoi announced it was willing to meet directly with Sihanouk, if China agreed to back only Sihanouk and drop support of the Khmer Rouge. In the announcement, the Vietnamese vice foreign minister said the key to solving the Cambodian issue was the withdrawal of Vietnam's forces from Cambodia and the exclusion of the Pol Pot regime.[36] A few days later, Hanoi was apparently having second thoughts about the prospect of direct talks with Sihanouk and reiterated the primacy of the four Cambodian factions deciding the fate of Cambodia by themselves.[37]

Hanoi's apparent flip-flop on the issue of direct negotiations nevertheless left open the possibility that Vietnam could be approached and perhaps convinced that direct talks were desirable. Vietnam formally announced the cocktail party would be held in late July, and that it would participate in the second phase of the meeting. The agenda was to include the planned Vietnamese troop withdrawal, the post–pull out scenario, refugee, and other bilateral issues. Despite the importance of these issues to Hanoi, there was no indication that Vietnam was interested in taking a more direct role in the consultations.[38]

With prospects of a settlement in the wind, the focus now turned to China and the Khmer Rouge. What could be done to ensure that the KR would not return to power? The question was the prominent one to the Vietnamese, and was equally important to ASEAN as well. Thailand doubted Vietnamese intentions to actually withdraw permanently from Cambodia, and other nations indicated that the prospects of Pol Pot's regime coming back to power were perhaps more undesirable than the regime they had been trying to oust for nine years.[39] Beijing argued that the Khmer Rouge would not come back to power by themselves. Instead, representatives from all factions would have a role in deciding Cambodia's fate through the electoral process.

Despite China's attempts to set minds at ease, the Khmer Rouge threat was deemed great, as they represented the best trained and well-equipped fighting force in the CGDK and were unlikely to give up their weapons. The *Washington Post* reported that China would offer asylum for Pol Pot and his aides, but Beijing denied the report as "unfounded and inaccurate (though it did say it favored a quadripartite coalition under the leadership of Prince Sihanouk).[40] While asylum for Pol Pot's group appeared in doubt, the statement and others like it suggested China was trying to elevate Sihanouk's role as the prospects for a settlement improved. The Chinese continued their support for direct talks between Sihanouk and Hanoi, despite Vietnam's rejection of the offer.

As the cocktail party drew nearer, the CGDK issued a statement suggesting points it considered relevant for the talks. It called on Vietnam to leave Cambodia in three phases under international observation. After the second phase, a quadripartite government should be formed to include the Phnom Penh regime and led by Prince Sihanouk. This government would be entrusted with organizing free elections under international supervision, and would also be in charge of writing a new constitution to secure Cambodian economic, financial, social, educational, cultural, and press institutions.[41]

China also suggested areas that would not only increase the

likelihood of a Cambodian settlement, but improve Sino-Soviet ties as well. The Soviet Union was told bluntly by the Chinese that prospects for a Sino-Soviet summit in 1988 depended on a swift Vietnamese withdrawal of troops from Cambodia. The Soviets, anxious to meet these demands, reportedly tried to pressure Hanoi to move toward this end. This prompted Vietnamese Foreign Minister Thach to ask Washington to work toward an independent Cambodia that would not present a problem to Vietnam—a move probably intended to bring American pressure on the Chinese to cut off support for the Khmer Rouge.[42] While the United States expressed its desire for a limited role for the KR, Washington strongly emphasized its preference for a Cambodia that was totally clear of Vietnamese interference. Secretary of State Shultz further insisted that normalized Vietnamese-American relations depended on a complete SRV military withdrawal from Cambodia.[43]

In addition to China and the Khmer Rouge, Hanoi was concerned about other pressing matters as well that threatened its war effort. In 1986 and 1987 Vietnam was embarking on an economic experiment. With foreign cash reserves all but nonexistent, trade limited to a handful of countries, and agricultural production lagging far behind demand, Vietnam realized that major economic restructuring was in order. Farm reforms, similar to those in China, were implemented on a limited scale in order to stimulate production. Greater efforts were made to procure fertilizer, tractors, electrical energy, and insecticides. More attention was given to rooting out corruption within the party and government bureaucracies. Finally, a serious reevaluation of Vietnam's war effort prompted party chief Nguyen Van Linh to admit publicly that the war was a drain, both in terms of lives and the national budget, and that Vietnam must have every soldier out of Cambodia by 1990 in order to reconstruct the country.[44]

Despite these admissions, Vietnam's problems increased during the first half of 1988. In March Hanoi appointed Va Van Kiet as acting prime minister to replace the previous prime minister who had died in office. It was hoped that Kiet, considered a pragmatist who favored economic incentives to bolster production, would be able to help Vietnam strengthen its sickly economy. But by mid-July, Kiet was officially replaced by Do Muoi, considered more of a hardliner, and not quite as willing to offer incentives for production. The election of the new prime minister, however, was seen by some as an attempt to rid the Vietnamese system of official corruption and set Vietnam on a course of disciplined development.

On the whole, while Vietnam had opened up politically, the economic sector remained unchanged and perhaps worsened. Some Vietnamese openly praised the Chinese economic system and called on their government to change radically outdated policies that governed the Vietnamese economy.[45] The economic situation therefore forced Vietnam to rethink its military efforts in Cambodia.

On June 30, Vietnam and Phnom Penh announced that Vietnam had started the withdrawal of the 150,000 troops stationed in Cambodia. Vietnam promised that 50,000 would return home by January 1989, with the rest to follow, culminating in a total withdrawal by 1990. Vietnam had announced withdrawals on several previous occasions, but most experts agreed that it was then merely rotating personnel rather than reducing its actual troop strength in Cambodia. What made this withdrawal credible was the presence of journalists to witness the massive convoys on their way back to Vietnam and the removal of the Vietnamese military hierarchy from Phnom Penh.

With the pull out from Cambodia came news of what the war had cost Vietnam in terms of casualties. The Vietnamese deputy commander in Cambodia said upon his return to Ho Chi Minh city that 55,000 Vietnamese troops had been killed in Cambodia since 1977, with at least that many wounded. He stated 30,000 were killed in border clashes in 1977–78, while the other 25,000 were killed during the nine years of occupation in Cambodia. Another official reported that many of the deaths resulted from sickness, particularly malaria, and the army's inability to care for the sick and wounded.[46]

China's reaction to the Vietnamese pull out was predictably businesslike. The foreign ministry issued a statement outlining China's proposal for settling the Cambodian question. It consisted of the following four points:

1. The complete withdrawal of Vietnamese troops from Cambodia is the necessary first condition. This will enhance the prospects for a political settlement.

2. The establishment of a quadripartite coalition government under the direction of Prince Sihanouk, while Vietnam withdraws its troops.

3. After establishing the coalition government, a freeze should be put on the size of each army and all groups should refrain from interfering in the general election and political situation in Cambodia to allow the Cambodians to decide their own fate.

4. International supervision should be instituted over the Vietnamese pull out and general election. Cambodia should then emerge as an independent, neutral, and nonaligned country.[47]

The statement was significant for two reasons. First, China went on the record for supporting negotiations on the subject of the political settlement in Cambodia while Vietnam withdraws. Up to that point, Beijing had been so determined to get Vietnam out of Cambodia that it seemed that the question of a political settlement could not be discussed until Vietnam had completely left the country. Second, China was clearly seeking a political solution that would give prominence to Prince Sihanouk and limit the powers of the Khmer Rouge (and the Vietnamese puppet regime in Phnom Penh). How far the Khmer Rouge would go in supporting Beijing's call for seizing its military campaign was uncertain, though most analysts agreed that under the circumstances, it represented the only plan that had a chance to succeed. Reports circulated that Khmer Rouge leader Khieu Samphan was an acceptable future member of the coalition by top officials in Hanoi and Phnom Penh, but analysts were divided on whether he or "retired" leader Pol Pot was really in control of the KR.[48]

The Chinese believed that movement by the Vietnamese was made possible by pressure from the Soviet Union, in particular in accordance with the spirit of the Geneva accords intending to solve the Afghan question. It also cleared the way for an improvement of Sino-Soviet relations, though Beijing remained cautious.[49]

Hanoi was cautious too. On July 3, the Vietnamese criticized the proposed format of the cocktail party to be held later that month in Jakarta. Hanoi insisted ASEAN members had turned from the original principles of the meeting, as agreed upon a year earlier in talks with Indonesian Foreign Minister Mochtar. Hanoi rejected ASEAN's proposal for Hanoi to meet directly with the four Cambodian factions, stating that Vietnam would join in the second phase of the meeting with the other regional nations. In addition, Hanoi rejected China's four-point proposal as "an attempt to block the road to a peaceful solution to the Kampuchea issue," because of what Vietnam saw as a failure to curb the power of the Khmer Rouge.[50] The Vietnamese also called China's demand for a timetable for the Vietnamese withdrawal an absurdity.

Despite these criticisms, the proposed cocktail party, scheduled for July 25, received endorsement from the United States, ASEAN, Japan, and was supported behind the scenes by the Soviet Union. U.S. Secretary of State Shultz repeated a previous offer to Hanoi, stating that the United States was looking "forward to normalized relations with Vietnam in the context of a Cambodian settlement."[51] In an attempt to prevent the return of the Pol Pot regime to power, Shultz later reaffirmed the United States' backing for Prince Sihanouk, and the introduction of a UN peacekeeping force—a point often rejected by Vietnam and the Phnom Penh regime.[52]

In mid-July, Prince Sihanouk resigned once again as leader of the CGDK. Sihanouk stated that due to "reasons that are inconvenient for me to explain, I have decided to resign as president of Democratic Kampuchea."[53] It was unclear why the prince had decided to renew his call to quit. China had given Sihanouk the nod as its primary hope to lead the proposed quadripartite coalition of Cambodia. It is possible, however, that Sihanouk still felt limited support from the Chinese. The Laotian ambassador to Beijing claimed Beijing's support to Sihanouk was mostly verbal, while its support to the Khmer Rouge was primary. Arriving in Paris, however, Sihanouk cited Khmer Rouge attacks against his forces as his primary reason for quitting as leader of the CGDK.[54] It is probable that Sihanouk was once again trying to rally support from all of his "allies," Khmer and Chinese, before attending the cocktail party.

The Jakarta "Informal Meeting"

The cocktail party, or as it was officially dubbed, the Jakarta Informal Meeting (JIM), began on a stormy note. On his departure from France to Indonesia, Norodom Sihanouk renewed his pledge to boycott the talks, adding that he was only going to Jakarta as a guest of the Indonesian president. Sihanouk vocally attacked the KR, explaining that his resignation from the coalition was meant to weaken and isolate the Khmer Rouge. He also argued that only China and Thailand had the power to prevent the KR from returning to power, by stopping arms shipments enroute to the Khmer Rouge.

Despite Sihanouk's resignation as head of the CGDK, his close associates continued to participate in the coalition and attended the talks in Jakarta that began on July 26. Sihanouk's people renewed the prince's call for a UN force to monitor the Vietnamese pull out and to make sure that the KR did not usurp power. Hun Sen revealed his own peace plan that called for a "national reconciliation council" to be headed by Prince Sihanouk. The council would supervise elections, while the Phnom Penh government continued to rule Cambodia until the elections were completed. The proposal was immediately rejected by Sihanouk's group and by the Khmer Rouge, but the impasse did not keep the talks from continuing.[55]

The second day of the JIM saw modest progress in two areas.

The first was a mutual agreement among Cambodian guerrilla factions and Phnom Penh and Hanoi that the Khmer Rouge must not return to power, and that all Cambodian groups must unite to form a single transition government. The main stumbling block to a solid agreement, however, rested on what to do with the Khmer Rouge, and how to deal with the KR's suppliers, the Chinese. Sihanouk's group again forwarded the idea of an international peacekeeping force, but the idea was rejected by Phnom Penh and the Vietnamese. Without one of the groups compromising on the issue, the talk process seemed doomed to failure.

On the third day of the talks, Prince Sihanouk ended his self-imposed boycott and joined in the talks. The prince blamed Vietnam and the Khmer Rouge for the root of the problems in Cambodia and argued that only he could ensure a successful peace solution in Cambodia. At the same time, however, Sihanouk dropped his insistence on an international peacekeeping force for Cambodia. The move appeared to be a concession directed to Hanoi (and possibly the KR) in order to move the talks along. He also indicated that if a quadripartite coalition government was organized in Cambodia, the existing Phnom Penh civil service could continue to function. Sihanouk's suggestions were weighed by those involved in the talk process, but disagreement arose over what type of international group should be organized to monitor the Vietnamese pull out and supervise the election process in lieu of a UN force. In addition, the Khmer Rouge expressed its strong aversion to Phnom Penh administering coalition policies.[56]

The last day of talks ended on a down note. Despite the fact that there was no lasting agreement made at the JIM, most of the factions involved seemed positive during the talks. The point of contention blocking progress continued to boil down to a dispute on the future of the Khmer Rouge. Phnom Penh suggested an agreement could be made on Cambodia's future that would exclude the Khmer Rouge. The Khmer Rouge attacked Phnom Penh as Vietnam's stooge and accused the other groups of giving in to Hanoi's demands. All in all, observers increasingly recognized that what was missing was a definitive Chinese statement on what their future support would be for the Khmer Rouge. Beijing remained quiet throughout the talks, reporting on them as an interested bystander, but did not hint of an impending change in policy toward the KR, thus contributing to the impasse at the JIM.

Despite the conflict of the last day of talks, Hun Sen and Sihanouk agreed to meet again in October, and a working group was organized to study the possibility of future talks similar to the format of the JIM. But the focus at this point shifted to the Chinese and their upcoming meeting with the Soviets to determine what could be done to limit the role of the Khmer Rouge.

From the JIM to the Paris Peace Talks

In the days following the JIM, most factions agreed on the necessity to distance themselves from the Khmer Rouge. This was especially true of Prince Sihanouk who stated that it was his belief that the gap between him and the Heng Samrin regime was closing,[57] and that Pol Pot's Khmer Rouge had "committed worse crimes against the Cambodian people than those committed by Hitler's Nazis against the Jews . . . ."[58] In an attempt to rob the KR of legitimacy, Sihanouk announced his intention to quit the CGDK's United Nations seat because of the dominant role the KR played in the CGDK. Sihanouk argued that to "accord legitimacy and state legality to the Khmer Rouge professes a deep and intolerable scorn for the Cambodian people."[59] The prince also stated that his group and Heng Samrin's troops would fight the Khmer Rouge, adding that he had international support for such an action.

Sihanouk's harsh criticism of the KR was successful in putting both the Khmer Rouge and Beijing on the defensive. Forced to legitimize themselves, the KR announced that following a political settlement it would reduce the size of its army to the same level as that of other factions.[60] At the same time, Beijing tried to downplay the future role of the KR to that of a political participant only. The Chinese stated that if any single Cambodian faction were allowed to exercise power by itself, or were excluded from the government, "it would be detrimental to achieving peace in Cambodia." They argued the greatest danger, however, would be "exercising power by the Heng Samrin–Hun Sen faction alone," thus maintaining their hard-line stand against Hanoi and Phnom Penh.[61]

Privately, however, the Chinese and the Khmer Rouge knew they were not convincing in their arguments. In talks with the Soviets, the Chinese recognized that the Khmer Rouge posed a danger in Cambodia and admitted that steps needed to be taken to check its role in a future settlement. The Khmer Rouge announced its willingness to participate in any meetings that sought to find a political solution to the Cambodian problem.[62] KR leader Khieu Samphan's statement clearly reflected a desire on the part of the Khmer Rouge to appear more conciliatory and diplomatic while distancing itself from its violent past. But while Khieu Samphan emphasized diplomacy, the Khmer Rouge started a new military offensive in what observers felt was an effort to give them clout at the bargaining table. Others felt the offensive was intended to give them territory within Cambodia for the day it would leave its Thai sanctuaries.[63]

Sihanouk's efforts to drop UN recognition of the KR met a snag. ASEAN managed to change the wording of the standard UN resolution on Cambodia (which condemned the invasion and occupation of Cambodia by Vietnam), by adding a clause resolving to prevent a return to power by the Khmer Rouge.[64] The resolution was passed, thus maintaining pressure on Vietnam to withdraw, and retaining the CGDK's status as the official government recognized by the United Nations. Thus Sihanouk's attempts to isolate the KR diplomatically within the walls of the United Nations was for the most part unsuccessful.

While Beijing tried to patch up the latest KR-Sihanouk dispute, the prince continued firing his anti–Khmer Rouge barrage, accusing them of attacking his forces and of committing atrocities against Cambodians along the Thai-Cambodian border.[65] By mid-October, however, Beijing's patience with Sihanouk had run out. The Chinese severed aid to his army as a result of Sihanouk's diplomatic offensive that was openly critical of Beijing and the KR. Sihanouk announced he was satisfied with the end of Chinese aid because, in China's absence, other countries were providing aid that would be used against the Khmer Rouge after the Vietnamese withdrawal.

An October follow-up meeting to the JIM failed to make any substantial progress because of the absence of the KR. Behind the scenes, Beijing pushed Khieu Samphan into accepting an international peacekeeping force as part of a Cambodian settlement—a point previously rejected by the Khmer Rouge.[66] But while the Chinese still believed a military role for the KR in a Cambodian settlement was desirable (and perhaps inevitable), Phnom Penh believed the Chinese-backed Khmer Rouge should be limited to a minor political role.[67] Still, the acknowledgment of a political role for the KR by Phnom Penh was a significant concession. But direct input from the KR continued to be absent, even in a meeting among Sihanouk's group, the KPNLF, and the Phnom Penh regime, held in France in early November. The process deadlocked and threatened to break down completely.

In an effort to save the talk process, Indonesia began to push for a second ministerial-level meeting to follow the progress of the JIM. Indonesian Foreign Minister Ali Alatas sought ways to ensure the participation of the KR, recognizing that any lasting agreement must meet with its approval, if a lasting peace were to be won. But the KR continued its efforts on the battlefront and chose to remove itself from the diplomatic process believing that as long as it abstained from the talk process, it would not suffer a defeat in a future settlement.[68]

In an attempt to take the diplomatic offensive, Sihanouk released a five-point proposal for solving the Cambodian question. This included: (1) a timetable for the removal of Vietnamese troops from Cambodia; (2) simultaneous dissolution of the CGDK and the Phnom Penh regime; (3) general elections supervised by an international team; (4) formation of a four-part provisional government and army; and (5) the presence of an international peacekeeping force in Cambodia.[69] The Khmer Rouge initially withheld comment on the draft. But the Chinese moved for direct KR participation in the talk process. Phnom Penh also took a noticeably softer line against the KR, indicating that Khieu Samphan had changed from what he had been twenty years earlier and could therefore take an active part in the negotiation process.[70] In addition, KPNLF leader Son Sann argued that "what happened in the past should be distinguished from what happens in the present and what will happen in the future," a statement intended to downplay the past role of the KR and focus on the Vietnamese presence in Cambodia.[71]

The change of attitude among the various parties in the talk process resulted in a pledge on behalf the KR to accept Sihanouk's five-point peace plan. But the KR was also reacting to a flurry of diplomatic activity between Beijing and Hanoi. As the Chinese became more convinced that Vietnam was serious about its withdrawal from Cambodia, and with ties improving between Beijing and Moscow, the Chinese took steps to upgrade relations with Vietnam. This resulted in a pledge to decrease military support for the KR, as Vietnam removed troops from Cambodia.[72] The Chinese further linked the reduction of aid to Soviet cooperation on the issue, believing that a Vietnamese withdrawal was greatly enhanced by Soviet pressure on Hanoi.[73]

Sihanouk seemed worried about China's pronouncement to reduce aid. He stated that China would not stop its assistance to the resistance until all Vietnamese troops were withdrawn. Sihanouk's troops were once again receiving aid from China which the prince wanted to continue, though he did not support the continuation of China's aid for the KR.[74] Nevertheless, Sihanouk was forced once again to walk the line between the Khmer Rouge and Beijing. At a banquet given in his honor by the Chinese, Sihanouk downplayed the atrocities of the KR and focused on the role of the Vietnamese in the conflict.[75]

As the second JIM drew near, the CGDK met together for the first time in eighteen months and outlined its strategy for the meeting. It called for a 2,000-man UN supervisory force to monitor the Vietnamese withdrawal and to keep the Khmer Rouge from taking power once the Vietnamese left. It also agreed to freeze its military forces to a ceiling of 10,000 soldiers within two months of the withdrawal and place them under the command of Prince Sihanouk. The Chinese seemed to go along with the plan, and praised Sihanouk for his efforts and leadership capabilities. But Sihanouk was still deeply suspicious of the KR and its overwhelming power compared to the strength of the other two factions in the CGDK.[76] He stated he would reject any role for Pol Pot and still felt the KR was guilty of numerous crimes, but admitted that isolating it would impede the reconstruction of Cambodia.

Once the second JIM got underway in Jakarta, the issue again came down to what to do with the KR. Despite Chinese assurances that their support for the Khmer Rouge would lessen as Vietnam withdrew from Cambodia, Phnom Penh continued to object to a military role for the Khmer Rouge and a political role no matter how small. Sihanouk attempted to break the impasse by reluctantly sticking up for the KR and condemning the role of Hanoi in the Cambodian problem. After six days of talks, the second JIM was over, having only discussed the issue of the Vietnamese withdrawal and the cessation of military aid to the various factions, but with no firm understanding on either issue. Khieu Samphan stated that the KR had decided that the realities of the situation mandated power sharing, free elections, and a ban on the participation of hard-line KR leaders. But his concessions were not enough to break the stalemate.[77]

At a mid-March meeting in Beijing, the various opposition factions decided that they needed to show greater unity in their dealings with Phnom Penh. In order to demonstrate this, they announced that Prince Sihanouk had been put in charge of all military forces of the CGDK.[78] Despite this pronouncement, the Vietnamese and the Phnom Penh regime knew that only the Khmer Rouge leaders themselves made decisions for KR armies. Sihanouk once again found himself weakened by the battlefield capabilities of the Khmer Rouge, which in turn undercut his political attempts to reach a settlement.

Prior to the May Sino-Soviet summit, Sihanouk seemed more willing to go along with Phnom Penh on various issues. In meetings with Hun Sen, the prince agreed that it would not be absolutely necessary for Phnom Penh to completely dismantle its regime after Hanoi's pull out. In turn, Hun Sen made a symbolic attempt to keep the talk process alive by unveiling a new flag to represent all of the Cambodian factions, proclaiming Buddhism to be the official religion, pledging to end capital punishment, and renewing an offer to give Sihanouk a high government post. China-Vietnam relations were improving as well. In addition to the restoration of trade across the SRV-PRC border, anti-aircraft batteries were pulled back, the Chinese introduced a Vietnamese specialist to serve as new ambassador to Hanoi, and Vietnam began using ethnic Chinese to rebuild the economy.[79] But the Khmer Rouge rejected cease-fire proposals put forth by Hun Sen and Sihanouk, citing the continued Vietnamese presence in Cambodia and their illegitimate Phnom Penh clients as reasons for its displeasure with the cease fire.

China's domestic political turmoil prevented Beijing and Moscow from creating a detailed strategy toward Cambodia during their May summit. Both sides agreed that upcoming talks in Paris should be attended by all parties involved in the Cambodian situation. Aside from this, little effort was exerted to discuss the matter further. For their part, the Chinese probably wanted to see if the Vietnamese were serious about a pull out, and Moscow considered its immediate responsibility completed with the normalization of relations with China. Indeed, China claimed that the Soviets had put adequate pressure on Hanoi to remove its troops, but the situation did not change because of Vietnam's continued occupation. The subsequent June violence at Tiananmen Square in Beijing took further momentum away from the settlement process, as the Chinese leadership concentrated on putting its domestic house in order.

As the August Cambodian peace talks got underway, all of the

Cambodian factions, as well as the Chinese, Vietnamese, Soviets, Americans, and other international actors expressed hope for a settlement on Cambodia. To this end, Sihanouk was forced to show unity with the KR at the talks with Phnom Penh and Vietnam. This spoiled the progress made between Sihanouk and Hun Sen months before, and gave the Khmer Rouge a bargaining position that Phnom Penh and Hanoi were uncomfortable with. In addition, all three of the superpowers, supporters of rival factions, left the talks after the first few days, further limiting the potential of the talk process to come to come up with options for ending the stalemate.[80] As a result, each side blamed the other for the impasse, and the Paris talks ended in failure.

By the end of September, large numbers of Vietnamese troops did leave Cambodia. China, however, did not end its military support for the Khmer Rouge, claiming Vietnam's withdrawal was only a partial one. The focus turned again to the battlefield, where the vacuum left by Vietnam was rapidly being filled by military forces of the CGDK, particularly those of the KR. Phnom Penh began conscription raids, and forced-drafting young men in market places, schools, and in their homes. Sensing that the diplomatic initiative had lost ground, Sihanouk called for a Cambodian UN trusteeship to bring order to the country. A few weeks later, Australian Foreign Minister Gareth Evans built on Sihanouk's idea, calling for the establishment of a UN transitional government in Cambodia, leaving vacant the Cambodian seat in the UN, and setting up an international supervisory body to monitor the total withdrawal of foreign troops from Cambodia, preside over a cease fire, and supervise general elections.[81] Sihanouk and the KR objected to the proposed surrender of the UN seat, while China reserved specific comment on the proposal.

The international initiative was resumed in January 1990 by the superpowers in another round of peace talks in Paris. Drawing on the various proposals from previous meetings, the Paris conference agreed on the following points:

1. A withdrawal of all forces (to be monitored by the UN) and cessation of outside military assistance.

2. The establishment of a transitional government, headed by the UN

3. Creation of a special representative to oversee and represent Cambodia at the UN.

4. The holding of general elections to replace the transitional government.[82]

The agreement had Beijing's support, but lacked specific endorsement from the four Cambodian factions. Sihanouk believed the conference had some merit, but focused his efforts instead on working out an agreement with Hun Sen. The two of them agreed to set up a Supreme National Council (SNC), suggested earlier in the Australian plan, to symbolize the unity and sovereignty of Cambodia. But details of the agreement never came to fruition. The Khmer Rouge refused to participate in the SNC because the council was to be comprised fifty-fifty of Phnom Penh and CGDK representatives, thus giving the KR significantly less representation than its Vietnamese-backed enemies. It is also likely the KR did not want to forward the CGDK interests as much as it did its own interests. The Chinese did not intervene in the process and stood by both the KR and Sihanouk, despite the obvious contradiction this created in their official policy. By May, hopes for a cease fire and creation of a Cambodian council were fading.[83]

In an effort to keep the SNC proposal alive, Sihanouk proposed making the council a body having equal representation from all four factions. But his proposal raised the same objections that Vietnam (and Phnom Penh) had to similar proposals that called for a four-part temporary authority in Cambodia. The SRV also rejected the idea that the SNC could have legislative power as an interim government. Beijing criticized Hanoi's objections to the plan, but failed to pressure the KR to accept the earlier proposal of equal representation for the Phnom Penh and CGDK regimes, even though it was accepted by the other members of the CGDK.[84]

By mid-July, most parties involved in the diplomatic process recognized that new ideas were needed. The KR military machine was moving closer to Phnom Penh, raising the fear that the

KR may soon return to power. In a surprise move, the United States dropped recognition of the CGDK UN seat, and agreed to talk to Vietnam about the Cambodian stalemate. Sihanouk expressed anger at the U.S. move, as did ASEAN. China voiced its regrets, knowing that the diplomatic shift, minor as it was, put greater pressure on Beijing to reconsider its support for the KR. As expected, Phnom Penh and Hanoi welcomed the move. Washington's shift was perhaps a quiet admission that its recognition of the CGDK represented tacit support for the Khmer Rouge. Hope was expressed in some corners that the UN seat could go to the SNC. But the United States immediately downplayed the significance of its diplomatic move in acknowledgment of ASEAN and Chinese protests, giving Beijing more breathing room, and removing the immediate hope that it, too, would reconsider its support for the Khmer Rouge.

Analysis: The Prospects for Peace in Cambodia

In mid-August 1990, the Khmer Rouge military continued to close in on Phnom Penh, yet Beijing's two-track policy continued. And while no single explanation will suffice to answer why the situation remains deadlocked, Beijing has certainly played a major role in leading Cambodia into the current stalemate.

Beijing's overarching concern has been, and continues to be, one of regional security. Chinese-Vietnamese relations have been strained for 2,000 years. The Sino-Soviet split accentuated the rift between Beijing and Hanoi, and coupled with Hanoi's hegemonist desires in Indochina, led to China's invasion of Vietnam in 1979. While there is no doubt that stronger ties between Moscow and Beijing will temper relations between China and Vietnam somewhat, there is still much room for rivalry. Chinese and Vietnamese efforts to gain the upper hand in Cambodia are the primary point of conflict between the two, while the Sino-Vietnamese border/territorial dispute, the problem of ethnic Chinese living in Vietnam, and other areas of competition add ferocity to the conflict, thus prolonging the impasse in Cambodia.

To be sure, China is not pleased with Sihanouk or the Khmer Rouge. The Chinese have used Sihanouk and the KR as tools needed to realize its goal of a region not dominated by Hanoi. This has presented several serious problems:

1. Chinese support for the KR has weakened Sihanouk's diplomatic efforts. The KR's military power has kept it on the battlefield and away from the bargaining table. Without the Chinese the KR was likely to have run out of material support in its war against the Vietnamese, and would not have been the strongest military force opposing Hanoi. In the absence of PRC support for the Khmer Rouge, military support for Sihanouk and Son Sann's KPNLF would most likely have been more forthcoming from the international community. This would have made negotiation with Phnom Penh easier, because of a weakened KR component and a greater military force backing the other members of the coalition. In addition, Sihanouk's role in the settlement talks have been seriously curtailed by Beijing's insistence that the KR play a role in negotiations and a future settlement. This has caused ASEAN countries and the outside world to view the situation negatively because of the possibility for a return to power by the KR.

2. Chinese support for Sihanouk and the Khmer Rouge (and the KPNLF) has failed to decrease factionalism within the CGDK and has probably increased the likelihood of disaster as direct Vietnamese intervention lessens. Thus the prospects of a civil war are great, considering the huge cache of weapons held by the Khmer Rouge and rival armies, and a lack of political unity needed to secure a peaceful settlement to the situation. Despite claims of a unified CGDK government, Sihanouk holds no real power to represent any group in the coalition other than his own loyalists. Furthermore, the KR has continued to be a militant organization that has demonstrated little political moderation within its organization or in working with other members of the CGDK or the Phnom Penh regime. Indeed, the KR is clearly viewed as the primary threat to peace now, not Hanoi or Phnom Penh.

3. Despite the strong possibility of civil war mentioned above,

even a divided Cambodia is likely to be seen in a more positive light to Beijing than a unified Cambodia closely aligned with Vietnam. This increases the possibility of not just civil war, but of the "Lebanization" of Cambodia, as different factions make competing claims within the country, each in turn seeking aid from various capitals outside of Cambodia.

4. It is possible that the KR could accept the fifty-fifty power-share plan between the CGDK and Phnom Penh if Beijing were to agree to back the measure. Despite China's claim to support the UN's efforts in Cambodia, the Chinese leadership has never considered cutting back its assistance to the Khmer Rouge in a serious way. Without Beijing's commitment, it is unlikely that the KR can be expected to go along with any power-sharing agreement that places Hun Sen's government on equal footing with the CGDK. Washington's dropping of recognition of the CGDK because of the legitimacy it gave the Khmer Rouge is a step that Beijing needs to consider if the Chinese are to construct a streamline policy that is free of the contradictions that have stalled settlement efforts in the past.

There is a possibility the situation could be resolved in another way. This could come about either as a result of moderation from all parties, particularly the Khmer Rouge, or through military victory for the KR, the Phnom Penh regime, the CGDK, or one or two CGDK members. A military victory will not come easily to any faction. But military conflict seems likely, given the failure to reach a compromise throughout the talk processes.

Thus the prospects for peace in Cambodia seem rather remote at the moment. The Chinese have, in part, what they sought. They have a Vietnamese pull out and an almost certain decline in Vietnamese influence in Cambodian politics. Beijing's two-track gamble has proceeded rather painlessly for China. Only in recent years did the international community express concern for Beijing's unwavering support for the Khmer Rouge. This policy, wrapped in the facade of support for Norodom Sihanouk, coupled with China's "coming-out party" since renouncing isolationism in 1978, helped maintain unity among members of the international community both within and outside the walls of the United Nations. Thus the Vietnamese remain the aggressors in the Cambodian quagmire, and the Khmer Rouge remain the strongest threat to long-term peace. China has thus far managed to escape blame.

5

Further Entanglements:
The Border/Territorial Dispute

Studies indicate that over 100 countries have disputed territories or borders.[1] With such a large number of conflicts worldwide, it is no surprise that such phenomena can entangle any number of nation-states. Indeed, the China-Vietnam conflict represents only one territorial dispute directly involving Beijing and Hanoi. Both capitals have additional trouble spots along their borders with other countries or in territorial waters where various governments have made competing claims of ownership. The following table provides a summary of the various territorial conflicts currently involving the two nations under study.

Though the current border and territorial disagreements between China and Vietnam constitute a significant challenge for the two countries, they do not represent the most serious contention between them. The purpose of this chapter, however, is to present the major tenets of the border/territorial disputes, and suggest how these factors have led to the worsening of Sino-Vietnamese relations.

The first part of this chapter will cover the border disputes and subsequent negotiations between Hanoi and Beijing. We will look at the historic boundary between the two nations, the Sino-French treaty of 1887 which contains the technical description of the current border, and reasons why the border is disputed. The

Table 5.1

Territorial Disputes Involving China and Vietnam

Nation	Dispute with:	Type
China	Soviet Union	Border
China	Mongolia	Border
China	India	Border
China	Japan	Territorial*
China	Vietnam	Border/Territorial
China	Philippines	Territorial
China	Malaysia	Territorial
China	Indonesia	Territorial
China	Taiwan	Territorial
Vietnam	China	Border/Territorial
Vietnam	Kampuchea	Border/Territorial
Vietnam	Philippines	Territorial
Vietnam	Indonesia	Territorial
Vietnam	Malaysia	Territorial
Vietnam	Taiwan	Territorial

*Territorial disputes refer to sea bed, island, and continental-shelf conflicts.
Source: Compiled by author.

second part of the chapter examines the territorial sea conflicts involving China and Vietnam and, to a limited degree, other countries which have competing claims to the territories. A summary and conclusion will follow that analyzes some possibilities the future holds for the border/territorial conflict.

The Sino-Vietnamese Border Dispute

Physical Description

The boundary between China and Vietnam passes through a geographic area of great complexity. On the western side of the boundary from Laos to Lao Cai on the Red River elevations reach in excess of 6,000 feet (see map 2). The area is characterized by high plateaus overlooking valleys of limestone and sandstone. On the eastern ranges, the elevation of the mountains and

Map 2. The PRC-SRV Border

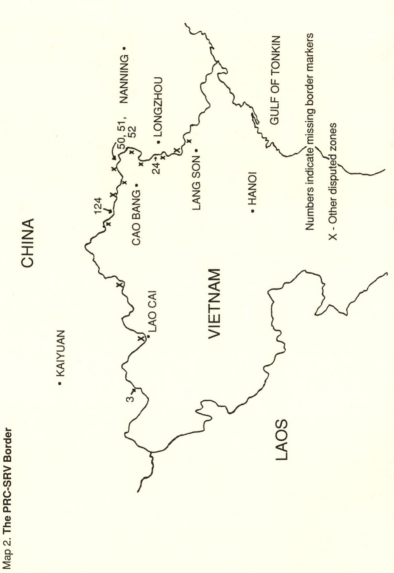

Sources: Office of the Geographer, Bureau of Intelligence and Research, U.S. Department of State, *International Boundary Study No. 38;*
China-Vietnam Boundary, December 15, 1978; National Geographic Society, *Asia,* map 02812, 1978.

hills is significantly lower, but is still rather rugged to the narrow coastal plain near the Gulf of Tonkin.

On the coastal plain and in larger valleys along the border, the native vegetation (comprised mostly of rain-forest varieties of trees) has been removed and replaced by rice paddies. In these areas, very little of the original natural vegetation can be found. Along the border areas, however, much of the native tree cover remains.[2]

The border itself is approximately 796 miles long. It begins at the tripoint of Laos and extends to the northern distributary of the Pei-lun Ho on the Gulf of Tonkin. The boundary follows drainage lines for about 506 miles, follows the median line of rivers for about 351 miles, is carved along straight-line sections for 23 miles, and the remainder of the boundary follows ridges, hills, and cultural features.[3]

The mountains between China and Vietnam have a low population density of about one person per square mile. In contrast, the river valleys around Lao Cai and Long Son have densities of about fifty persons per square kilometer. Generally speaking the density along both sides of the border ranges between eleven and fifty persons per square kilometer. Most of the population along the border is employed in agriculture, in particular paddy rice, though there are a significant number of garden farms that grow sweet potatoes and corn.

The area along the Sino-Vietnam boundary is inhabited almost entirely by ethnic minorities. Only in the extreme east near the Tonkin Gulf do Han Chinese constitute a significant proportion of the population. The west is inhabited primary by the Akha and Ha-ni (Tibetan-Burmese) peoples. Only in the Red River valley is there a significant number of Vietnamese. The remaining areas are inhabited by Miao, Yao, and Tai minorities.[4]

Two railroads cross the border. The Hanoi-Kunming route runs between the Gulf of Tonkin on the Vietnamese side to China's Yunnan Province. A second route runs from Vietnam to China's eastern rail net at Ping-xiang. Several roads cross the border including: (1) a coast road, (2) through Friendship Pass near Long Son, (3) between Cao Bang and Jingxi, (4) between Cao Bang and Na-po, (5) between Ha Giang and Wen-shan, (6) and along the Hanoi-Kunming railroad. The Red River is also navigable to Man-hao in Yunnan Province.[5]

Carving the Border

Until 207 B.C., the land currently lying in South China and North Vietnam used to be an area populated by independent tribes and small kingdoms. It was then that the Han dynasty incorporated this area into its borders. The actual boundary line has fluctuated, depending on the strength of the central governments in China and Vietnam. It was not until the French began to exert considerable influence in Indochina that the need was felt to establish permanently an internationally recognized boundary. Thus on June 26, 1887, a Sino-French treaty was signed, marking in principle the present-day boundary between China and Vietnam.

Though both sides claim that they adhere to this boundary as agreed upon by the Sino-French treaty, disagreements remain as to where the actual borders lie. A major reason for this confusion can be found by referring to the language of the treaty itself. The document lacks the detail and specificity needed to describe accurately the boundary divisions. For the most part, the treaty was laid out by reference to a map, following the confluence of rivers, or by connecting imaginary points on the map. As is evident from this type of delineation, interpretation is subject to wide speculation.[6] With many small rivers cutting new courses, and the ever-changing drainage patterns of the watersheds, the boundaries as indicated in the treaty have changed from what they were in 1887, or they were never defined carefully enough in the first place.

The difficulty in following the actual borderline is evident from the following U.S. State Department description of the boundary:

> . . . the boundary is most complex. For approximately 75 miles the

boundary extends generally northeastward along minor watersheds. However, it crosses the Riviere Claire 1.5 miles northwest of Thanh Thuy and then the Song Mien before joining the Chin Chiang at the northernmost point on the boundary. . . . For about 60 miles, minor drainage divides from the line although the Song Gam cuts the boundary at pillar 129. After a 10-mile segment determined by straight lines and other non-physical features near Sac Giang, the boundary again consists of drainage divides for about 55 miles. Exceptions are made as three minor streams cut the boundary.[7]

With the ever-changing drainage systems of the watershed, confusion has arisen between the two countries as to where the actual border between the two countries lies. In a SRV foreign ministry statement on March 16, 1979, Vietnam claimed China had taken advantage of changing river flows to encroach upon Vietnamese territory:

> The Hoanh Mo fording in Quang Ninh Province was built in 1968 with Chinese aid . . . the medial line of the river was honoured by both sides. . . . But as China . . . had built only one water culvert close to the Vietnamese bank, the current shifted its course totally toward the Vietnamese side; then the Chinese side moved toward Vietnamese territory. This trick was also used in regard to the Po Hen fording (Quang Ninh), and the Ai chanh dam (Cao Bang), and the Ba Nam Cum bridge (Lai Chau) . . . .[8]

The Chinese side has rejected the claims that it has taken advantage of shifting rivers and has instead claimed that border problems have arisen since Vietnam began an anti-China policy and began militarizing the border areas as early as 1975. Until that time, China argues, border disputes were handled by local authorities.[9]

A second major problem along the border of China and Vietnam is the presence of stone border markers. The markers were originally placed to mark the boundary where natural physical landmarks could not be used. The problem with this is that there are approximately 300 pillars in seven areas, intended to designate the boundary in thirty-mile strips.[10] There is very little agreement by the two nations as to where these markers were originally sitting when the treaty was signed and whether or not the other side has in fact moved the markers for convenience. The SRV argues that China has repeatedly moved the markers inside Vietnamese territory to take productive agricultural lands and to expand its control over Vietnam.[11] The PRC maintains the markers were either moved by the Vietnamese authorities or are in fact resting in their historical places.[12]

All told, the area in question ranges anywhere from a few kilometers in Quang Ninh Province, Vietnam, to thirty meters of railroad track at Friendship Pass near Long Son. From the sources available it is evident that part of the dispute could stem from the fact that the pillars are few and far between, thus making a clear judgment as to the actual location of the border difficult. Second, with the changing nature of the landscape, it is possible that farmers have moved the markers to suit the demands of agriculture. At any rate, the apparent loss of territory seems to be more of a problem for Vietnam than China, as China has made no claims of having lost territory to Vietnam along the boundary.

Another source of conflict along the borders has arisen from the economic activities of the peoples living in the border areas. Joint Sino-Vietnamese work projects seem to have been areas of contention for some time. Vietnam has felt that many of the work projects were done in a way as to benefit the Chinese side to the loss of the Vietnamese side. An example of this was made clear in the March 1979 SRV foreign ministry statement cited above. According to Hanoi, Beijing has continually used its influence in proposing projects along the borders to move the boundary to China's favor. This allegation stems from disagreements after work projects were begun to construct bridges, dams, pipelines, roads, and rail lines. China has rejected this claim, stating that China and Vietnam were able to work together well in the construction of these projects and that both sides benefited from the projects.[13]

On the other hand, China claims Vietnam has used its own projects to take Chinese territory. Beijing argues that three islands were taken by the Vietnamese in Xiaobazi, Yunnan Province, when Vietnamese authorities built a dam changing the directional flow of a river's main channel. Vietnamese armed personnel then drove away the remaining Chinese citizens and took the land for Vietnam.[14]

Vietnam accuses China of borrowing agricultural lands in assisting with agriculture inside Vietnam's borders, then afterward falsely claiming that the land has historically been China's.[15] China rejects such accusations and instead asserts that such claims reflect Vietnam's anti-Chinese policy and are a further attempt to cover up Vietnamese infractions along the border.[16]

The presence of ethnic Chinese living in Vietnam also agitates the situation, as the SRV claims the PRC repeatedly uses the Han population in Vietnam to carry on anti-Vietnam espionage and sabotage activities. This will be handled in more detail in the next chapter.

Border Negotiations

Since the border war of February–March 1979, there have been negotiations held at irregular intervals between China and Vietnam. These negotiations have been held in part to discuss the border problems. But there has been no sign of progress in this area. Despite pledges of entering the talks with good intentions by both sides, neither government has made significant efforts to get beyond name calling and symbolic attempts to settle the issues. There are several reasons for this:

1. The language used in provisional drafts by both governments in seeking to address the issues along the border has been confrontational in nature. All documents presented claim the other side is solely to blame for the border difficulties. In fact, there is no common agreement as to what are the issues at stake.[17]

2. There are other issues that clutter the border disagreement. The territorial sea dispute also relates to the border dispute, as it too calls upon reference to the Sino-French treaty of 1887 for a description of the boundary between the two nations. The language in that document is vague on this matter as well, making certain interpretation impossible at present.

3. The ethnic Chinese population also poses a problem. In

some regions it constitutes a significant share of the population, thus making clear distinction between Chinese and Vietnamese territory difficult.

4. Vietnam's incursion into Cambodia dominates the current Sino-Vietnamese conflict. The border dispute thus constitutes a problem of lesser importance to Beijing and Hanoi. This is not to say that border problems do not add significantly to the strife between Hanoi and Beijing. Hanoi especially feels the heat from the border dispute, but has learned to read the struggle in direct relation to its activities in Cambodia.[18]

5. Vietnam and China's relationship to the USSR also has a bearing on the border dispute. China looks to Vietnam as a close client state of the Soviet Union and therefore has to negotiate border problems with overall Soviet activity in Asia in mind. This is less true in the relationship of the two capitals toward Washington, though there is some hint that China may have originally perceived support from Washington for the border war of 1979 before it invaded.[19]

6. Finally, the snail-like progress in talks on all of the issues mentioned above indicates that Hanoi and Beijing have agreed to talk more out of perceived need than out of genuine willingness to seek answers to stinging problems. While this phenomenon has perhaps prevented the occurrence of another large-scale "lesson" being "taught" to the Vietnamese by the Chinese, it has not produced any significant negotiations leading toward lasting peace.

With these complications cluttering the border conflict, resolving the problems at present is next to impossible. Progress in border discussions can only be seen in terms of a larger improvement in Sino-Vietnamese ties in the other areas mentioned above. This is also true to a great extent with the territorial sea conflict. We shall now turn to an analysis of this problem.

The Territorial Sea Conflict

There are principally three areas in the South China Sea that are disputed by China and Vietnam. The first is the Tonkin Gulf region where the PRC and SRV cannot agree on where the national borders have been officially demarcated. The second area is the Paracels, an archipelago southeast of Hainan Island, and the Spratlys, a chain east of Ho Chi Minh city. In addition to China's and Vietnam's disputing claims to the islands, other nation-states in the region also maintain that they have a legal ownership to all or part of the islands. In recent years, the promise of oil deposits in and around these islands, and in the continental-shelf regions of the Gulf of Tonkin, have increased the relative importance of the islands both to the PRC and the SRV.

Physical Descriptions of the Territories under Dispute

The Gulf of Tonkin is that area of the South China Sea immediately south and east of the easternmost border shared by China and Vietnam (see map 3). It lies between China's Hainan Island and the Vietnamese mainland. The water depth in the gulf ranges from around 60 feet to 300 meters, making it attractive for offshore oil exploration. The gulf is fed by many rivers, the largest being the Red River (which flows from China, where it is known as the Yuan, through Vietnam, where it collects the waters of other large rivers before emptying into the gulf).

The Paracels are 150 miles from the southern coast of Hainan Island, and 240 nautical miles from Da Nang, Vietnam. Vietnam, China, and Taiwan all claim the islands, though China has maintained complete control of the island group since 1974. The archipelago consists of two groups, the Amphitrite group and the Crescent group. In total the two groups contain about fifteen islets and several major sand banks and reefs. The Paracels are known to the Chinese as the Xisha (Western Sand) Islands, and to the Vietnamese as the Hoang Sa (Yellow Sand) Islands.

The Paracels were used in the past as a source of guano, tropical fruits, some lumber, fresh water, and an area excellent for commercial fishing. The main interest for the Chinese in recent years has been for oil exploration and in maintaining an

Map 3. The Disputed Islands

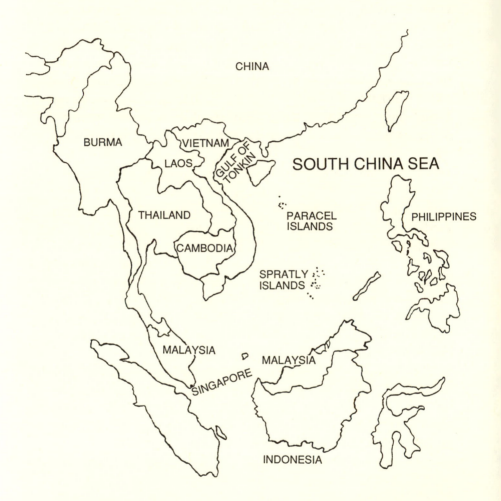

Sources: Office of the Geographer, Bureau of Intelligence and Research, U.S. Department of State, *International Boundary Study No 38: China-Vietnam Boundary,* December 15, 1978; National Geographic Society, *Asia,* map 02812, 1978; Ministry of Foreign Affairs, Republic of Vietnam, Saigon, *White Paper on the Hoang Sa and Troung Sa Islands,* Saigon, 1975; Ministry of Foreign Affairs, People's Republic of China. "China's Indisputable Sovereignty Over the Xisha and Nansha Islands," *Beijing Review,* February 18, 1980, pp. 14–24.

offshore base to monitor the sea traffic of the South China Sea.

The Spratly archipelago extends over 1,000 kilometers from north to south. It is approximately 650 kilometers east of the Vietnamese coast, 1,000 kilometers south of Hainan Island, 160 kilometers west of the Sarawak (Malaysian) coast, and 100 kilometers west of Palawan Island (Philippines). Several countries have made claims to all or part of the Spratly archipelago. The entire archipelago is claimed by China and Vietnam, though the PRC has no representation on the island chain today. Vietnam has maintained control of seven islands in the archipelago for several decades, the Philippines has held six islands since 1971, and a ROC (Taiwan) garrison has held the island of Itu Aba in the chain since 1949. Malaysia has also made claims to the islands in the past, but seems to have been less vocal on the matter in recent years.

There are four principal groups in the Spratly Islands. The Western Spratlys contain approximately thirty small islands, reefs, banks, and shoals, and is where most of the more significant islands are located. The Southern Shoals make up the second group of islands, and is mostly comprised of small reefs and shoals. The Dangerous Area, the third group, is comprised of shallow reefs and rocks. Most of this area is uncharted and is avoided by ships and fishermen due to the hazards of navigating in these waters. The final group, the Eastern Spratlys, consists of eleven islands and reefs, and is controlled almost exclusively by the Philippines. Of the four groups, only the Western Spratlys have proven to be of significant economic worth. The islands in this group have supplies of fresh water, grasses, trees, guano, and significant oil deposits are believed to lie in the shelf area around the islands. Fishing is abundant in all four groups.

The Spratlys are referred to by the Chinese as the Nansha, or Southern Sands. The Vietnamese call the archipelago the Truong Sa, or the Storm or Tempest Islands. All of the individual islands in the four groups have been given both Chinese and Vietnamese names.[20]

Evolution of the Conflict

The Tonkin Gulf

The major obstacle in the Tonkin Gulf dispute centers around determining where the historical treaty of 1887 between the French and the Chinese intended the Sino-Vietnamese boundary to be and whether or not that boundary is acceptable to both sides. Indeed there is no clear reference to the Gulf of Tonkin in the text of the treaty itself. A later agreement between the French and the Chinese allowing for trade between China and Annam mentions a few general details about the Tonkin Gulf, but the references there only deal with the issuance of permits and policing boat traffic on the gulf.[21]

In 1977, both sides agreed to meet on the issue of determining the borders of the Bac Bo or Bei Bu Gulf, thus suggesting there had been problems in determining where the official boundary was. (Bac Bo is what the Vietnamese refer to as the northern area of the Tonkin Gulf where this dispute is centered; the Chinese refer to it as Bei Bu.) Though the details of the discussions are not available, it appears the dispute focuses in part on certain aspects of the twelve-mile territorial sea limit and 200-mile economic sea limit as discussed in the United Nations Third Law of the Sea Conference.[22] Both the SRV and the PRC have pledged support to the technical aspects embodied in the Law of the Sea, but the problem of where the boundary actually exists in the Tonkin Gulf continues to cloud agreement as to where SRV claims end and PRC ownership begins and vice-versa.

There are claims that Chinese territory begins at longitude 108 degrees east. If this is so, then the Vietnamese would receive two-thirds of the waters in the gulf, and the Chinese would receive the Paracels. This is considered unacceptable to both the PRC and the SRV, as both sides want all of the disputed claims for themselves.[23] Both the foreign ministry statement of the SRV of March 16, 1979, and the speech delivered by Chinese Vice-Minister Han Nianlong on May 12, 1979, at the Sino-Vietnamese peace talks mentioned the dispute surrounding the boundary in the Tonkin Gulf, but no specifics were mentioned from either side.[24] This is probably because the dispute over the Tonkin Gulf has been overshadowed by the disagreements over the island groups. But its importance must not be underestimated, especially since both sides have repeatedly fired on boats drifting into disputed waters, and since both sides have moved their oil exploring activities closer to disputed waters. Since the dispute in the gulf began in earnest in 1978, both sides have tried to stay clear of the other's waters in order to prevent a major ocean conflict.

Though there is not a great deal known about the details of the Bei Bu or Bac Bo Gulf dispute, we can summarize generally about the situation:

1. The boundary dividing the territorial waters of the PRC and SRV is not clearly defined. Part of this is because the language of the treaty and subsequent documents discussing the area is vague. Much of the treaty referring to the gulf refers to imaginary points on a map, rather than to distinct physical aspects of the gulf. Second, due to the proximity of the Vietnamese and Chinese mainlands to the disputed waters, neither side is willing to chance giving up waters that are considered to be important in terms of security.

2. The conflict looms larger due to the overall deterioration of relations between the PRC and SRV. The number of disputes rose sharply when problems arose such as the expulsion of ethnic Chinese residents from Vietnam and Vietnam's invasion of Cambodia. In recent years, particularly since 1975, the gulf has become more important to both countries due to the prospect of exploiting oil resources in the region.

3. The Law of the Sea provides mechanisms for dealing with disputes, but the above disagreements do not necessarily address the possibilities of resolving territorial problems as envisioned by the UN convention.[25]

4. Finally, the Tonkin Gulf dispute is overshadowed by other aspects of the Sino-Vietnamese conflict, as well as other territo-

rial conflicts that receive more attention from Hanoi and Beijing. There is also the absence of any third party either involved or affected by the conflict. This does not hold true for the other territorial conflicts.

If agreement should be made on other border or territorial issues between the two capitals, most likely it will be reflected in a decrease in incidents and rhetoric concerning the northern end of the Tonkin Gulf.

The Island Archipelagos

In many respects, the disputes surrounding the island archipelagos are better understood than the Tonkin Gulf dispute. This is in part because more information is available on this subject, and perhaps because both sides are more specific on their rights to claim the islands—indications that they are perhaps of greater overall importance to the two sides than the Tonkin Gulf dispute.

History plays a prominent role in the argument over the Paracels and Spratlys.[26] In the postwar era, conflict over the islands first became an issue in the late 1950s. The Paracels and Spratlys were claimed by the Chinese government on June 15, 1956, on the basis of historical ownership. According to the PRC, Vietnamese Vice Foreign Minister Ung Van Khiem received Li Zhimin of the Chinese embassy and told him that "according to Vietnamese data, the Xisha (Paracel) and Nansha (Spratly) Islands are historically part of Chinese territory." This claim was, in Beijing's view, acknowledged by an article which appeared in the Vietnamese Communist Party newspaper *Nhan Dan* on September 4, 1958, after the Chinese foreign ministry made official claim to its territorial seas that included the Paracels and Spratlys. Similarly, the Chinese claim Vietnamese Premier Pham Van Dong on September 14 of the same year wrote a note to Zhou Enlai stating that "the government of the Democratic Republic of Viet Nam recognizes and supports the declaration of the government of the People's Republic of China on China's territorial sea made on September 4, 1958 . . . ."[27]

In making its case for ownership of the islands, the SRV until early 1988 relied extensively on the actions of the former Saigon administration of the Republic of Vietnam (South Vietnam) as justification for claiming ownership. On January 18, 1982, the SRV Ministry of Foreign Affairs issued a white book on the Spratlys and Paracels. Hanoi refers to the actions of the Saigon regime in taking steps toward securing the islands as legitimizing, in part, its claim to the islands. The SRV states that the ROV (Republic of Vietnam, or the Saigon government) took over the islands after the French left Vietnam in 1956. The ROV later placed the islands under the jurisdiction of provinces and placed sovereignty markers on the islands. It later reaffirmed the ownership of the islands to be Vietnamese in 1971.[28]

On January 15, 1974, the PRC decided to challenge Saigon's claim to the Paracel Islands. PRC gunboats attacked the small South Vietnamese garrison stationed on the Paracels and put a permanent hold on the archipelago. It is not clear what kind of resistance was put up by the Saigon regime, or what the immediate reaction was from Hanoi, but Beijing attempted to mask the incident as a matter of Chinese self-defense, arguing that they were attacked first and that they were merely making a claim to territory that had historically been China's.[29] Though it is probable that Hanoi did not make it public at the time that it disapproved of China's actions, the SRV has made it clear since 1978 that the act angered the SRV.

On April 19, 1975, it was reported that the Provisional Revolutionary Government of Vietnam had taken some sand bars and reefs in the Spratly archipelago. The islands were held by the faltering Saigon regime, but the act was perhaps more significant because it marked an open challenge to Beijing for sovereignty over the islands.[30] There was no immediate response to the incident from Beijing, though the Chinese probably had held some of the same feelings that Hanoi held when China took the Paracels a year earlier.

Before continuing, it is important to look at some of the reasons why there seems to be an apparent contradiction about what

Hanoi authorities were saying about the island archipelagos in 1958 and what they were saying by 1978. To begin with, during the late 1950s Vietnam was looking for support from the PRC. It was willing to give a great deal to ensure that China would remain its close ally during the growing unrest in Indochina. This was in part why Hanoi was willing to give in to Zhou Enlai's demands at the Geneva conference of 1954, and in turn, to surrender two seemingly insignificant archipelagos in the South China Sea. The Vietnamese civil war and growing U.S. involvement in the region meant Hanoi needed Beijing's support. The islands could not be a point of disagreement for endangering the future relationship with Vietnam's larger neighbor. When the U.S. threat decreased, and reunification of Vietnam became a reality, the desire to reclaim the islands gained a new priority on Hanoi's agenda.

Though it is possible that the PRC has exaggerated the complicity of Hanoi in 1958 in acknowledging the islands as PRC territory, still it is evident that Hanoi did in fact at least make token overtures to appease the Chinese on the issue. In fact, the SRV has avoided mentioning the agreements in 1958 between the two countries in regard to the islands and refers instead to the PRC's confusing the islands in question with other islands.[31]

With the February war of 1979 barely concluded, the foreign ministries of both countries began issuing detailed historical accounts to gain the upper hand in claiming ownership to the islands. Vietnam made the claim that since the 1700s Vietnam had had economic interests in the islands, and had used the archipelagos for commercial gain.[32] It also asserted the French acknowledged this claim early on during their activities relating to the colonization of Indochina.[33] China argued, on the other hand, that its historical claims to the islands went back 2,000 years. It claimed to have documented through various journals and books that in fact the Chinese had declared ownership to the island groups long before the Vietnamese had any real knowledge of their existence.[34] In 1979 the Chinese published maps and documents to further their claims to the islands. Reinforcement followed through an impressive document released by the Ministry of Foreign Affairs on January 30, 1980, wherein evidence was presented linking China to the islands as early as the second century B.C.

This document published names of books and official logs containing the names of the different islands, reefs, and sands comprising the Paracels and Spratlys. The document refers to the history that unfolded on the islands in terms of government projects that were set up, commercial interests that were in operation, and archaeological artifacts that were uncovered, confirming Chinese people inhabited the islands in past centuries. The document also claims that the French took the islands not from Vietnam, but from China, as recorded in various French volumes that describe the archipelagos under question. The ministry included photomechanical reprints of maps published by the Vietnamese government for use in school textbooks and official capacities acknowledging Chinese ownership of the islands. In all, the package presented by the PRC Ministry of Foreign Affairs gave Beijing the upper hand in the propaganda battle.[35]

It was not until 1982 that Hanoi was able to offer a substantial challenge to the Beijing claims. In January of that year, a series of six articles were published in the *Vietnam Courier*, followed by the white book on the Vietnamese claims, which offered insight into the Vietnamese position on the issue.

Hanoi argues that missionary journals, maps, and books clearly indicate Vietnamese ownership of the islands by the 1700s. But it is possible, Hanoi argues, that the Vietnamese had had earlier contact with the islands, but the Chinese dynasties destroyed all of the major historical volumes belonging to Vietnam. Particularly mentioned were the abuses of the Chinese to the Vietnamese during the fifteenth century when the Chinese burned major historical works in order to bring Vietnam under Chinese domination.[36] It is argued that records were kept of various expeditions during the fifteenth century to the islands. The Vietnamese indicate that not only did they travel to the islands, but they attempted to introduce agriculture on the islands—thus establishing Vietnam as the first country firmly to put down roots on the islands.

Hanoi dismisses Chinese claims to the islands as groundless. It argues there is no clear indication that the islands being referred to in Chinese literature are in fact describing the islands under question. As to the artifacts found, Hanoi has posited two explanations. First, Hanoi accused Beijing of making up the story of archaeological evidence found on the islands, claiming that it could have uncovered the artifacts anywhere and simply used them to fabricate a story about its origins to the islands. Second, Hanoi holds that if artifacts have been found on the islands, they cannot be construed of as a claim of ownership, but are explained as having been transported there much the same as Japanese swords from the third century are found in China, or Roman coins from the second century A.D. are found in Vietnam.[37]

The bulk of Hanoi's claim came from the French notes and studies that were made on the island archipelagos during the period of colonization. It argues that such records cannot be equaled by the Chinese, and that therefore real interest in the islands came later to the Chinese. Many of these records are scientific studies done on growth of the reefs, analysis of guano deposits, and surveys of botanical and marine life made by the Vietnamese and French authorities as far back as the late eighteenth century and early nineteenth century. Hanoi's white book more or less restates the claims made in the *Vietnam Courier*, except in an abbreviated form, as it does not answer as many of the Chinese claims. Many of these claims, in turn, were first made by the Saigon government in a white book it released on the same subject in 1975.[38]

Although Hanoi's initial argument was perhaps not as impressive as Beijing's, it was still premature to declare a winner in the island debate. Neither side lodged a truly convincing argument to support its overtures for ownership of the islands. In addition, various factors complicate the issues. These factors perhaps are the overarching reasons that both sides so desperately want to control the islands. I will now turn to a discussion of these factors.

Security Issues. Regional and global power factors have made the area of the South China Sea grow in importance in recent decades. A large portion of Asia's trade, and the world's trade for that matter, passes through the South China Sea.[39] As regional and global powers grapple for footholds in the region, the South China Sea stands as a staging ground for nations to make their presence felt. In recent years, nations have begun to extend their navies to ensure that a proper balance is maintained. As the Soviet naval presence increased in Vietnam, the United States, China, the Philippines, Indonesia, Malaysia, and Thailand sought to meet that challenge by increasing the visibility and strength of their armed forces. For China, offsetting the Soviet and Vietnamese influence in the region has become a top priority.

The Chinese began accusing the Vietnamese of inviting the Soviets in to build bases as early as 1978. The Vietnamese denied the charges, saying that Cam Ranh Bay served only as a stopping ground for Russian vessels and as an area to unload needed aid from the Soviet Union. But it soon became apparent that Chinese fears were warranted. Portable docks and military facilities were confirmed by U.S. intelligence sources, who saw the facilities as the first permanent Soviet base off the Soviet mainland.

China agreed to visits from the American secretary of defense, and began to discuss weapons purchases with the United States. Finally, in 1986, American warships began making port calls to Chinese cities, the first since 1949.[40] Against this background, the islands have become more important.

The Paracels provide China with an outpost to watch Soviet naval activities in the South China Sea by extending the Chinese presence an additional 200 miles from the mainland. In addition to the island outpost providing a buffer area for the Chinese mainland, it also serves as a deterrent to the Vietnamese war machine by providing the Chinese with another area to stage punitive naval strikes against the Vietnamese.[41] Perhaps most important, the Chinese military presence on the Paracels is a symbolic effort, attesting to Beijing's determination to oppose further encirclement by hostile neighbors.

The Spratlys, held by the Vietnamese, are no immediate threat to the Chinese. In fact, it is curious in many respects that China continues to claim the Spratlys as a vital issue. The island archipelago is closer to Malaysia and the Philippines than it is to Vietnam and China. There is, perhaps, a potential for any nation that controls the Spratlys to be in a position to control, to some degree, the shipping lanes in the South China Sea. This may not, however, be the case, due to the poor mooring prospects and precarious waters in which the Spratlys lie. The Vietnamese do, however, fear encirclement by the Chinese. As one analyst put it, the real significance of the contested areas is not for territory, but as a bargaining chip for future negotiations between China and Vietnam.[42]

In early 1988, however, fierce fighting erupted between Vietnamese and Chinese gunboats in the Spratlys. Following the discovery of petroleum deposits several months earlier under the Spratly chain, China significantly beefed up its military presence in the islands. This led to naval confrontations between the two countries, and led to seventy Vietnamese deaths.[43] Vietnam's quick defeat in the clash prompted Hanoi to ask China for talks to end the fighting. Moscow also encouraged discussion between the two Asian capitals so as not to derail Moscow and Beijing's path of improved relations.[44]

In late April, Hanoi presented its most articulate argument supporting its claim to the disputed Spratly and Paracel chains.[45] The Vietnamese referred to customary international law in forwarding its claims of ownership. Hanoi argued:

1. The right of first discovery of territories does not constitute the right of occupancy.

2. Occupation of territories by private individuals does not constitute territorial sovereignty.

3. Occupation by conquest does not entitle a nation-state to sovereignty over conquered territory.

To support these views, Hanoi carefully argued that China's claims were falsely based on the above three points. Hanoi claims that Vietnam has a right to the islands based on France's return of the island territories to Vietnam under the provisions of

the 1954 Geneva agreements, which were subsequently backed
by international law. But Hanoi's claims did not impress Beijing,
nor Manila, Kuala Lumpur, and Taipei. All four capitals made
competing claims to the islands, with Taipei suggesting it would
join forces with the PRC to keep the islands part of Chinese
territory.[46]

Vietnam reacted by increasing troop strength on the islands it
was holding, and the Chinese stated they had decided to send
marines to "defend the nation."[47] In addition, China announced
plans to build an air traffic control center on one of the regions'
disputed islands. Though the center, according to Japanese officials, was needed, it was likely the move was to support China's
claims to the island chains.[48]

China's growing presence in the Spratly and Paracel chains
did not constitute a major buildup, but was probably meant to
strain Vietnam's already overheated military budget. Beijing's
decision to move its navy into the Spratlys could have been in-
tentional, in order to coincide with growing pressure on Vietnam
to end its occupation of Cambodia.

Oil Potential. When the Republic of Vietnam reported that it
had an oil strike on the coast of Vietnam in 1975, the importance
of the Tonkin Gulf and the Paracels, and to a degree the Spratlys
also, increased in the eyes of Hanoi and Beijing. Vietnam is an
energy-dependent importer, receiving most of its oil supplies
from the Soviet Union.[49] Similarly, by the late 1970s and early
1980s, oil production of onshore Chinese reserves had begun to
decline, making the drive to drill offshore imperative to avoid
costly oil imports.

Shortly after Vietnam was reunified it was estimated that there
were three or four offshore oil rigs working in shallow waters in
the Tonkin Gulf. But in 1984, it was learned that probably only
two were actually working.[50] After some apparent disappointments, the Vietnamese-Soviet drill crews discovered their first
major producer in April 1986 in the Bach Ho (White Tiger) field,
seventy-five miles offshore, between the port of Vung Tau and

Kon Dao Island.[51] The Chinese had forty rigs in service in 1984, twenty-six in 1985, and thirty-two in 1986.[52] Of the sixteen Chinese rigs operational in the South China Sea, four were drilling in the Tonkin Gulf, with actual production to begin in 1986.

Though both sides have experienced disappointments in the actual production of oil, the prospects still seem positive for developing oil reserves in the gulf areas. The promise of oil production has increased the tension in the region, especially between Vietnam and China. Not only is the northern end of the Tonkin Gulf considered a rich field, but the Paracels also show signs of oil beneath its seas. Oil potential between Hainan Island and the mainland of Vietnam is considered fair (1–10 billion barrels) to high (10–100 billion barrels). The oil potential south of Hainan Island and surrounding the Paracels is also considered fair to high. Until late 1987, the Spratly potential was largely unknown and unexplored.[53] But in mid-November 1987, China announced it had discovered rich oil and gas deposits under the Spratlys after a survey of 180,000 square kilometers. There was no immediate announcement of China's plans to exploit the deposits.[54]

As exploration and speculation over oil reserves increased, so did the tension over disputed territories. In 1979, Hanoi warned that if China continued to search for oil in the disputed waters in the Gulf of Tonkin, companies which took up those concessions would have to bear the consequences.[55] China was accused of "reservoir drilling," that is, pumping Vietnamese oil deposits by drilling on an angle to reach Vietnamese oil from Chinese waters.[56] Though the threats continued to mount, there was no effort to turn threats into action. In the event that a major discovery is found in highly disputed waters, it is likely that both sides may be more willing to act on those threats.

In early 1987 China attempted to bring its Tonkin Gulf wells into production.[57] Vietnam was also moving toward this end. The Chinese and the Vietnamese expressed great interest in expanding their exploration and drilling capacities, which in some cases meant considering companies which could end up with contracts with both the Vietnamese and Chinese.[58] In May 1988, a number of Western countries, including the United States, were being considered by Hanoi as possible partners to assist Vietnam's search for oil. The Vietnamese felt the Soviets were unable to exploit rich reserves in the Tonkin Gulf because of poor technology and techniques.[59] The introduction of more Western oil firms into the gulf raised speculation that Beijing and Hanoi would soften their territorial claims and try to cooperate more toward coordinating exploration and drilling activities. At any rate, the oil problem still has large implications in the territorial dispute. It is not likely that these disagreements will be solved in the immediate future.

A summary of the major tenets of the territorial sea conflict between China and Vietnam is in order. The negotiations which have been held to discuss the border dispute and animosities between the two nations have also been used as a forum to discuss the territorial sea problems. There has been no significant progress in solving this dispute. The reasons for this are principally:

1. There is disagreement as to what the treaties of 1887 and 1895 actually say about the Gulf of Tonkin region and the Paracel Islands. Because of this, there is no clear legal document to refer to in looking for a standard of reference from which to negotiate.

2. Interpretations of historical rights in regard to ownership of the Paracels and Spratlys vary greatly. Beijing's argument is somewhat convincing on grounds of historical contact with the islands over time. Vietnam's claim on the basis of developing the islands economically and performing technical studies is also marginally significant, if considered within the context of the French turning the territories over to Vietnamese control after colonization. On the other hand, both sides perhaps are grasping at weak evidence in an attempt to gain the upper hand in the conflict.

3. The islands under dispute have some strategic value, even if mostly for symbolic purposes. They have become such a sensitive issue that it would be considered a significant loss should the Paracels be taken from the Chinese, or the Spratlys from the

Vietnamese. Though the islands offer little in terms of increasing military might, they nevertheless perform a function in serving as an extension of their owners' regional influence. From the Paracels, China can, to a certain degree, watch over Soviet and Vietnamese activities in the area.

4. The prospects of finding oil in and around the disputed territories have greatly increased interest and tension in the conflict. Though the Spratlys at present offer no real potential, the Paracels and Tonkin Gulf regions are considered oil-rich. This has brought new meaning to the conflict and could lead to further problems of greater intensity than experienced in the past.

5. Finally, the territorial sea conflict is once again an indication of larger problems between Beijing and Hanoi. It was not until relations hit rock bottom in 1978 and 1979 that the territorial dispute was seen as a crucial problem dividing the two countries. Thus there is a danger in overestimating the significance of the territorial sea dispute if not taken in perspective with the other issues at hand.

Conclusion

It is likely that if there is to be any agreement made in addressing the border/territorial conflict between China and Vietnam, it will most likely follow an improvement of relations in other areas. The greatest obstacle that has divided China and Vietnam from 1975 to the present day has been the conflict over the fate of Indochina.

For now it is likely that border shelling will continue along the frontier regions of China and Vietnam, not necessarily out of a desire to gain ground on the other, but as an indication of poor relations generally. The territorial sea conflict will also continue to boil, again not because of any aspect peculiar to the territorial question itself, but due to competition between Vietnam and China on a variety of issues.

The main indicators to watch in the ongoing border and territorial struggles are matters that involve both nations generally. The disputes discussed here are seen as barometers, indicating the intensity of the conflict in all areas of Vietnamese-Chinese relations.

6

Ethnic Entanglements:
The Chinese in Vietnam

For most outside observers, the first serious signs of strain between Vietnam and China came in 1978 when Beijing expressed concern over the mistreatment of ethnic Chinese living in Vietnam. Before that time it was generally accepted that Hanoi and Beijing were not getting along as well as they had in the past. But the sudden explosion of words and diplomatic action surrounding the ethnic Chinese issue took many by surprise.

The mistreatment of overseas Chinese living in Vietnam did not present Beijing with the major reason to invade that country in February 1979. It does, however, constitute a major source of contention between the two nations. For a short while in 1978 almost all problems between the two countries were discussed in terms of the ethnic Chinese problem. Indeed, the expulsion of ethnic Chinese and the diplomatic tussle surrounding that dispute became a barometer for measuring hostilities between the two countries.

The purpose of this chapter is to discuss the underlying reasons for the conflict surrounding the ethnic Chinese dispute and how Hanoi and Beijing have sought to deal with this problem. First we consider the problem in historical terms. The presence of Chinese living in Vietnam has been a problem for some time, not just since 1975. In particular, the first section of this chapter reviews the situation in which Chinese living in Vietnam found themselves after 1975. Second, it is necessary to analyze the official handling of the problem by Hanoi and Beijing in an attempt to understand the issue in greater detail and assess the prospects for dealing with it in the future. The third section of this chapter will give an overview of the ethnic Chinese situation in Vietnam since the 1979 war. A conclusion follows.

The Ethnic Chinese in Vietnam

The genetic origins of the Chinese and Vietnamese peoples are largely unknown. Generally it is believed that the Chinese are more closely related to the Mongolian and Tibetan peoples. They are generally larger in stature than the Vietnamese, and their language groups suggest significant influence from the Asiatic mainland language groupings. Vietnamese are considerably smaller in stature and speak a language reflecting Malay/Burmese influence. Though these differences exist, the minority tribes of South China share some of the same bloodlines as the minority tribes of North Vietnam, and the Vietnamese in general. Because the two nations border each other, there has been a sharing of certain traditions of language and culture. But the Vietnamese have remained remarkably independent, as have the Chinese living in Vietnam, reflecting the strong cultural traditions of each nation.

Since the long history of relations between Vietnam and China has already been discussed, it is necessary only to analyze those particular areas of conflict in recent years that relate to ethnic Chinese living in Vietnam. The problem is more than just a difference in ethnic background between the Chinese and Vietnamese. Chinese have maintained networks of social, educational, and economic influence that until recently were left relatively untouched, despite far-reaching attempts by the Vietnamese authorities to limit their influence.

It is estimated that there were around 1.7 million ethnic Chinese living in Vietnam prior to the exodus of the late 1970s and early 1980s.[1] Most Chinese lived in the south of Vietnam, especially in or around the Saigon-Cholon (Ho Chi Minh City) metropolitan area. This is a significant increase in the numbers of Chinese residing in Vietnam from previous years. The estimates in 1937 placed the total number of Chinese living in Vietnam to be around 200,000, or about 4 percent of the population.[2] But there has not been a huge influx of Chinese moving into Vietnam since the 1920s. In fact, available statistics show that the immigration/emigration figures between China and Vietnam remained relatively stable until 1977.[3]

A great majority of the Chinese residing in Vietnam come from southern China, in particular Guangdong, Guangxi, and Fujian provinces. The most prominent dialect spoken in Vietnam among the Chinese is Cantonese, which is recognized as the market and trade language.[4] The vast majority of the Chinese living in Vietnam are involved in marketing, trade, transportation, and various industrial pursuits, though there are a fair number of Hakka Chinese living on the Vietnam-China border who carry on agricultural occupations.[5]

Most Chinese coming to Vietnam were invited by family members, or businesses on a preferred basis. In other words, in most cases, there were jobs waiting for the Chinese immigrants before they arrived. In many cases, they were filling positions of family members who were returning to China or accepting new jobs that had opened up as business conditions improved. Most Chinese were in Vietnam to carry on a needed trade that paid well. This is evident from the fact that Chinese generally made better wages than the majority of Vietnamese, and the Chinese always dodged attempts by the Vietnamese authorities to assimilate them into the mainstream of Vietnamese society.

The Chinese organized themselves into communities in Vietnam, much as they have done in other nations of Asia and other areas of the world. These communities are known as *bangs*. Within bangs, Chinese residents in Vietnam can carry on life much the same as they did in China. Bangs have an administrative apparatus which coordinates Chinese efforts to influence the

Vietnamese authorities and to establish rules of conduct within the Chinese communities. Bangs set up formal and informal rules for operating businesses and trade, and provide education for Chinese school-aged children, and in some cases legal advice and representation. At one time there was even a hospital and medical system for the Chinese that operated in Vietnam but refused treatment to the Vietnamese. All Chinese immigrants were subject to the rules of bangs, and infractions of the rules could result in punishment, in terms of fines or expulsion from a bang or from Vietnam itself.[6]

Bangs to some extent also fostered secret societies. Bangs in Vietnam and other Asian communities outside of China are shrouded in mystery and are associated with killer squads and other mob-type organizations. They have roots to many of the gangster-type organizations that flourished in pre-1949 China.[7] The dark side of these bangs has been a major reason for past attempts by the authorities in North and South Vietnam to curtail the activities of bangs generally, hoping that lessened political and economic influence would also limit clandestine strength.

By far the greatest influence felt in Vietnamese society from the Chinese bangs was in business. The close cooperation and organizational effectiveness of the organizations helped the Chinese gain the upper hand in many sectors of the Vietnamese economy. The Chinese managed, over the centuries, to capture the bulk of trade in agricultural commodities. The trade and transport of these commodities was controlled by bang cooperation.

The rice-husking and processing mills in Vietnam were principally owned by the Chinese. These millers bought grain from the rice traders, also Chinese, who owned the boats and carts to take the rice from the fields to the mills. Rice brokers, again Chinese, ran several levels of the rice business. Some brokers put millers and traders in touch with local Vietnamese farmers who had a crop to sell. They would negotiate a price and arrange for the shipping and milling of the rice crop. Once the rice was milled, brokers again entered the scene and worked as middlemen to find markets for the rice products. This resulted in more work for the

Chinese controlling the transport routes, who sold the rice to local Chinese marketeers and merchants. While rice was sold to the Vietnamese on the local markets, it, and other agriculture commodities, was also shipped overseas, again through the assistance of local bangs, and bangs in Singapore, Malaysia, the Philippines, and other nations having Chinese communities.[8]

Chinese moneylenders also found it profitable to operate in Vietnam. Money could be lent to local farmers and entrepreneurs, always promising a handsome return to the lender. Cooperation with a Chinese moneylender would almost always result in guaranteed business, because it provided a market to sell a crop through the cooperation of the Chinese brokers and rice agents. Though the principal area of Chinese economic strength centered around the rice markets, other industries were heavily dominated by Chinese as well. Fishing, mining, lumbering, trade of finished products, and so forth, all benefited from the existence of the networks already in place from the Chinese rice monopolies, and thus could use the existing channels for opening new areas of commerce. In most cases, this resulted in large portions of the economy being captured by the Chinese with barely any Vietnamese influence.[9]

Until 1956, 90 percent of all trade was controlled by the Chinese. In that year, the government of the Republic of Vietnam attempted to curb the influence of the Chinese businesses in Vietnam. The government passed a law ordering all Chinese to disband their monopoly on rice trade and other crucial sectors of the Vietnamese economy. The Chinese objected, and in so doing pulled their money out of the banks, asked other Asian Chinese communities to join in a blockade against Vietnamese products and trade, and fought opening up their family-run businesses to Vietnamese investment. The results were nearly catastrophic. The government suffered severe problems as the economy nearly failed with the absence of the Chinese contribution to the economy.

In order to halt the rapid decline of the economy, the government compromised and allowed the Chinese to continue their trades as long as 51 percent of their companies were Vietnamese-owned. Chinese families got around this law by having one or several of their family members take on a Vietnamese name. In short, the businesses were reorganized on paper, but in reality retained their ever-powerful status, just as they had before 1956.[10]

By 1960, 90 percent of all industry and commerce in North Vietnam was taken under public ownership. The Chinese were able to avoid a great deal of this collectivization at first, but later had to compromise to avoid open and dangerous clashes with the Hanoi authorities. But the Chinese were not totally powerless after cooperating with the government. Many Chinese were appointed to be directors of the state-owned industries and businesses that they used to own. The result was some success for the Vietnamese in assimilating the Chinese in the North, though the influx of Chinese into public service also meant continued Chinese influence in the economy.[11]

The government's desire to limit Chinese influence in the economy was echoed by the Vietnamese people at large. Although they tolerated the Chinese, and in many cases got along well with their Chinese neighbors, the Vietnamese still resented the power held by the Chinese and their bang societies. It was difficult for a Vietnamese business person to make a go of it in those areas of the economy where the Chinese were, because they would either fail, due to harassment by the Chinese, or would have to conduct their business affairs according to Chinese rules. Furthermore, consumer prices for a great many of the staples consumed in Vietnam were either totally controlled by the Chinese, or directly affected by the complex networks of trade and bargaining carried on by Chinese interests.

The 1970s brought major changes in Vietnam's approach toward ethnic Chinese. When it became evident that Vietnam would soon be reunified, Hanoi attempted to change the legal status of Chinese living in Vietnam. New identification and travel papers were issued to Chinese residents in Vietnam as a halfway step in the naturalization process. These moves were apparently accepted by Beijing, though the Chinese living in Vietnam disliked the new changes. After 1975, the issue of Chinese living in Vietnam became a heated problem. The government implemented anti-Chinese policies to be effected in the business sector once again. Collectivization and public ownership was announced which led to large-scale speculation, as the Chinese went underground to protect their businesses. The immediate result was inflation and hoarding of goods. By 1976, all Chinese were required to register with the government and were strongly encouraged to denounce Chinese citizenship and accept Vietnam as their official homeland. The moves were reinforced by a forced closure in September of that year of all Chinese schools and Chinese-language newspapers.[12]

In December 1976, the pro-China faction of the Vietnamese National Party Congress was purged in favor of the pro-Soviet faction. The switch was a signal that China and Vietnam were struggling in their relations and that Hanoi believed Moscow could offer more economic aid to the troubled Vietnamese economy. This resulted in more fear among the Chinese living in Vietnam, and led to further attempts to go underground with their businesses. Faced with economic difficulties, Hanoi implemented sweeping reforms in all areas of the economy. The results were especially drastic in the South, where the structure of all primary and secondary sectors of the economy was considerably altered. Chinese rice brokers, transport companies, and millers found themselves nearly ruined as a result of the economic reforms. The government forced ethnic Chinese and other minority groups living on or near the Chinese border either to emigrate to China, or to be forced into the government's new economic zones, located in those areas of Vietnam where capitalism "needed strongest reformation"—in other words, the South.

To Hanoi's dismay, the economy continued its downward turn despite the new attempts to build a strong centrally based system. The Chinese found new ways to operate on the black market, which to a significant degree nullified the attempts of the Communists to end the influence of the Chinese.[13] Once again, sweeping changes were introduced by Hanoi to bring the economy under control and to break up the strength of the Chinese businesses. In short, these policies consisted of the following:

1. The southern part of Vietnam was set up as a place for resettling populations from the North, and was to utilize the rich farmland to provide needed foodstuffs for the nation at large.

2. The state took an active role in attempting to take control of agricultural and industrial enterprises in the South which in many cases were owned by Chinese. This was done by confiscating lands and properties and setting up cooperatives to collectivize agriculture and industrial production.

3. When the above two policies failed to make the desired impact, the money system was reorganized, and those holding large amounts of cash under the old system quickly saw their savings reduced to a fraction of its previous worth. This especially hurt Chinese business persons who had lost faith in the banking system of Vietnam and held reserves in the old currency.

4. The Chinese were seen as a major obstacle to the reforms and therefore received considerable attention from the government and Vietnamese citizens at large. The Chinese were accused of being "counterrevolutionaries," and "dangerous capitalist elements."[14]

Two factors, more than any others, seem to indicate why anti-Chinese sentiment was so high by 1978. The first is that local Vietnamese were obviously tired of the stranglehold that the Chinese held on the various sectors of the Vietnamese economy. Despite the emergence of a socialist government and supposed defeat of the capitalist classes, the Chinese were able to keep their businesses running. The second factor is the huge negative balance-of-payments problem that Vietnam had been rolling up in its efforts to modernize. By 1980, Vietnam was U.S. $669 million in the red, largely from a growing trade and financial burden with the Soviet Union. In addition, the per capita income for 1979 in Vietnam was estimated at barely over U.S. $191, compared to $198 per capita in 1976.[15] Clearly Hanoi had been ineffective in bringing growth to an already weak economy. Radical reforms were seen as the only possibility to tackle the balance-of-payments problem and negative growth rate.

By the first week in April, 30,000 businesses had been closed in Ho Chi Minh City as a result of the new reforms. Official government accounts referred to the process as the "socialist transformation of the South."[16] But the "antibourgeois" campaigns were seen more as anti-Chinese campaigns and the refugee crisis began.[17] Chinese officials were not allowed to visit the Cholon area of Ho Chi Minh City. This raised the level of tension between Hanoi and Beijing, though both sides were hesitant to make their dissatisfaction known openly. Railway service along the Yunnan-Hanoi line remained open, and airline flights to Hanoi from Chinese cities remained on schedule. But it became clear that China could no longer hope that the refugee crisis would be short-lived.

Temporary housing and resettlement efforts were hampered by a lack of facilities and an overall shortage of employment opportunities for returning Chinese, even though several provinces were designated as official reception centers for the refugees. Many Vietnamese Chinese felt China could not offer them the type of opportunities they had realized in Vietnam, especially wealthy Cholon businessmen who chose to go to other countries by boat. Other Chinese did not have time to consider their options and chose to flee Vietnam to avoid being resettled in one of Vietnam's new economic zones, known for harsh treatment and forced labor.[18]

In early May 1978, China finally broke its silence and accused Vietnam of implementing an anti-China campaign and of forcing the emigration of Chinese citizens. Reports were received in several Asian countries that Chinese were killed in Cholon through government efforts or encouragement.[19] Hanoi denied the allegations and argued that the Chinese were in fact instigating anti-government riots in the cities and that the authorities and Vietnamese people were merely responding to the violence in an attempt to bring about order.

As the rhetoric between Beijing and Hanoi increased, so did the flow of refugees across the border into China, and onto boats leaving Vietnam for other Asian countries. Though the actual open signs of hostility seemed to evolve rather suddenly, it is important to remember that Hanoi had been struggling with the problem of the Chinese living in Vietnam for some time. In the years after reunification in 1975, the problem took on new proportions as 5.3 percent of the population in the South, or over 1,000,000 of the total population, were ethnic Chinese, who wielded enormous economic influence and fought against the socialization of the South. Chinese aid waned in the postwar years, and Hanoi found itself more reliant on Moscow for financial help. In short, pressures had increased to the point where a showdown between Hanoi and the overseas Chinese was just a matter of time. The showdown came in 1978.

Diplomacy and Debate

The first diplomatic shots fired in the dispute came through the press. These were brief but pointed remarks intended to blame the other for being the sole instigator of the dispute. On May 4, 1978, the Vietnamese foreign ministry made an official statement which blamed the Chinese side for enticing Chinese to leave Vietnam, by spreading rumors of impending war between China and Vietnam among the Chinese residents of Vietnam. This was followed on May 24 by an official statement from the spokesman of the Overseas Chinese Affairs Office in Beijing. The Chinese rejected Hanoi's explanation of the Chinese refugee crisis and instead cited Hanoi's anti-China policies based on several points:

1. Since 1977 Vietnamese authorities, in an effort to "clear the border areas" of longtime residents of Vietnam who were of Chinese ancestry, encouraged Chinese to flee to China or the new economic zones. This developed into the "massive expulsion of Chinese residents in all parts of Vietnam."

2. The Chinese people who returned to China were working-class people who were brutalized both physically and emotionally by the Vietnamese and not wealthy businessmen as Hanoi contended. From April to mid-May 1978, over 70,000 had returned to China.

3. After questioning the refugees returning from Vietnam,

China found the Vietnamese authorities had told the Chinese residents that China was asking them to return to China. Beijing argued that the Vietnamese did this to promote hostility and intimidate the Chinese residents living in Vietnam.

4. Vietnam forced Chinese residents to take on Vietnamese nationality against their will and went against the agreement reached in 1955 when Chinese and Vietnamese leaders met and decided the status of Chinese living in Vietnam. That agreement held that Chinese could change their nationality, and were encouraged to do so, but only according to individual desire and not by force.[20]

The Chinese took further steps in the first week of June. They suspended all aid projects to Vietnam and recalled the technicians and workers involved on the projects.[21] Though the ongoing projects involving the Chinese were considered limited compared to Soviet-assisted projects, the suspension still had far-reaching effects. China's aid to Vietnam from 1960 to 1978 was considered to be around 10 billion U.S. dollars, most of that before 1975. But Vietnam had a difficult time refunding and finding countries willing to complete the projects that China had started. By September 1978, COMECON countries had not been able to cover the eighty projects that were previously funded by China and seemed unwilling to make generous concessions to help Hanoi complete the projects.

Vietnam was also hurt by the exodus of Chinese residents who had held together significant sectors of the economy. Particularly hurt were the coal, fishing, shipping, and steel industries. Furthermore, new economic zones along the border areas of Vietnam were being abandoned by Chinese who refused to work under harsh conditions and preferred to take the risk of finding improved opportunities in other neighboring Asian states, or in the West.[22]

By the first of June, 90,000 Chinese had returned to China. Beijing, in an attempt to embarrass the Vietnamese, and to build world opinion against the Vietnamese, sent two ships to Vietnam to bring home ethnic Chinese.[23] The plan did not go as smoothly as Beijing had hoped, however. Hanoi was able to capitalize on the Chinese move and sent thousands to the docks where the ships arrived in order to pressure China into taking more than it could possibly handle. Hanoi's moves were intended to bring international attention to the fact that China's actions were a reflection of empty talk rather than genuine concern for the welfare of the Chinese people. Once the ships landed in Shanghai, many refugees refused to disembark, arguing that they wanted to go to a country where they could carry on with their businesses as they pleased—a factor which further tainted Beijing's propaganda campaign.[24]

Meanwhile, Hanoi was busy reinforcing border positions along the Chinese frontier. Tunnels were dug which enabled the Vietnamese to carry on clandestine sabotage efforts against the Chinese inside China's territory. It also continued to spread rumors of an impending invasion from China in order to keep up the rapid Chinese exodus. But Vietnam's side of the story was not favorably received among other Asian nations or the rest of the world. Nearly every day condemnation of Vietnamese activities was being voiced, as Hanoi was directly blamed for the huge exodus of not only Chinese residents, but for the refugee crisis in other areas of Indochina as well.[25]

China heated up its diplomatic attacks on Vietnam. The foreign ministry issued a statement reaffirming the points made previously by the Overseas Chinese Affairs Office and added that Chinese residents in Vietnam were not allowed to carry on in the economic affairs of Vietnam on an equal basis with the other peoples of Vietnam. The foreign ministry statement implied that the problem was tied to the slowdown of Chinese economic aid given to Vietnam after reunification in 1975. Beijing argued that Vietnam refused to show appreciation for the enormous sacrifice China made to give Vietnam aid in the past. After 1975, China could not afford to give additional aid, nor was it warranted, due to the fact that Vietnam was no longer at war. The statement made reference to a conversation that Zhou Enlai had with an unnamed Vietnamese leader, where Zhou supposedly explained China's position:

> During the war, when you were in the worst need, we took many
> things from our own army to give you. We made very great efforts to
> help you. The sum of our aid to Viet Nam still ranks first among our
> aids to foreign countries. You should let us have a respite and regain
> strength.[26]

The above statement is significant in that it implies that the
crisis involving Chinese residents in Vietnam is a reflection of
larger problems that developed between the two countries, especially since 1975. It is probable that Vietnam had expressed general dismay at the amount of aid that China had offered Hanoi in
the postreunification years. It also lends insight into why Vietnam began to lean toward the Soviet Union for assistance in
1976.

In an attempt to state its case amid widespread condemnation,
Hanoi began to issue statements explaining its side of the story in
greater detail and to refute the diplomatic gains China had made
in the refugee crisis. The Hanoi Press Service released a confession of an ethnic Chinese man who admitted to carrying out
anti-Vietnam policies in Vietnam under the direction of the Chinese government. In the confession, the man explained he was
contacted by a Chinese agent who wanted him to be a part of a
campaign to tell all Chinese in Vietnam that the motherland
wanted them to return to China to participate in the great rebuild-
ing projects. In his confession he states:

> This was to arouse national pride among the Hoa people. [Hoa is
> the official designation for Chinese peoples living in Vietnam.] Then
> we would propagandize about China's policy of solicitous concern
> for Overseas Chinese. The aim was to make the Hoa people in Viet-
> nam turn their thoughts toward China and become receptive to our
> urging to leave Vietnam and contribute to China's reconstruction
> with their manpower and wealth. . . . we had to point out that
> Kampuchea and Vietnam were conducting a war, that China whole-
> heartedly supported Kampuchea, that China and Vietnam would have
> great differences and that this situation would cause difficulties for Hoa
> people living in Vietnam. We were then to incite the Hoa people to
> demand the restoration of their Chinese nationality and return to China,
> bringing along all property for national construction.[27]

Once again, as the above quote suggests, other issues complicated the ethnic Chinese problem. But the refugee crisis served
as a focal point to express hostilities to each other generally.
Clearly the overall decline in relations contributed to the hysteria
and emotion of the Chinese problem. Had the other areas of
contention between Vietnam and China not existed, it is likely
that the issue of ethnic Chinese living in Vietnam would have
been handled very differently by both Hanoi and Beijing.

In July 1978, Hanoi attempted to rid itself of blame in the
refugee crisis by arguing that the refugee crisis was a result of
continued war and disruption from foreign powers and not due to
anything that the Vietnamese had done. In a lengthy press release, the Vietnamese authorities pointed to the external
challenges that Vietnam had faced in the past, leaving its industries in ruin and its people in poverty. The refugees, therefore,
were primarily fleeing poor economic conditions and not political mistreatment. An exception to this, however, were the Chinese residents in Vietnam who were considered by Beijing to be
"Overseas Chinese instead of a part of the Vietnamese nation."
China continued a policy of "big-nation chauvinism," in compli-
ance with the notion of the "great Han race of feudal China."[28]

Hanoi's charges were made in part with some justification.
Beijing has taken extraordinary interest in the overseas Chinese
in many nations and has sought their support from time to time to
arouse international support for China. China is perhaps one of
the only nations that considers its policies of importance not only
to Chinese living at home, but to those living abroad as well. In
addition, Chinese have found it preferable to carry on life in
closely knit Chinese societies wherever they live, even though
their residence may be away from Chinese soil. Such has been
the case in Vietnam, where Chinese loyalties have been to family, clan, surname, bang, and lastly government.[29] But even
though government support is considered of considerably less
importance to the Chinese living in Vietnam, this loyalty has
historically been directed primarily to the Nationalist Chinese
government in Taipei, and only second to the Communist gov-

ernment in Beijing. Hanoi's authority has not been a priority for loyal support among the Chinese in Vietnam.[30]

Hanoi contends this close-knit society, with implicit support from Beijing, meant that the Chinese were as much to blame for the lack of general economic development and overall conditions of poverty in Vietnam as were the U.S. imperialists in supporting the South Vietnam regime. Hanoi contends that before reunification 80 percent of the food, chemical, textile, and metallurgy installations, as well as the engineering and power industries, were owned by the Chinese. In addition, nearly 100 percent of the wholesale trade and import-export trade was controlled by the Chinese. In all, more thar "200 comprador bourgeois of Chinese descent and several industrial and trading bourgeois of Chinese descent firmly controlled the southern economy. . . ." Hanoi further argues that because of bang organizations, and through the support of the Chinese government for these Chinese who opposed socialist transformation, the Chinese have been able to disrupt and sabotage the Vietnamese economy.[31]

For China, the conflict by August had turned to a discussion of the legal status of Chinese residents living in Vietnam. Beijing reiterated that the Chinese living in Vietnam in the past were encouraged to change their nationality to Vietnamese, but they should not be forced to do so. Beijing also claimed that the Chinese living in Vietnam were told to respect local laws and customs, but that the Chinese government was "duty-bound to protect their proper rights and interests, and it is hoped that the countries concerned will also guarantee these rights and interests."[32]

Beijing said it assisted Vietnam in taking over Chinese schools and newspapers and encouraged the Chinese in Vietnam to decide whether to return to China or to take on Vietnamese nationality. According to Beijing, Hanoi made the mistake of harassing the Chinese, by forcing them to take Vietnamese nationality or be expelled from the country. The Chinese were fired from their jobs, ostracized, persecuted, and had their food rations stopped.[33] The direct result was inhumane treatment and 160,000 Chinese residents deported to China—causing economic hardship in China's resettlement efforts.

For the remainder of 1978, relations remained tense as both Vietnamese and Chinese troops amassed along the border. When China invaded in February 1979, one of the reasons first mentioned officially by China for "teaching Vietnam a lesson" was the harsh treatment Chinese living in Vietnam had received by the Vietnamese authorities. In the war's aftermath, and in subsequent diplomatic exchanges, new developments emerged revealing the complexity of the refugee crisis and the mistreatment of Chinese living in Vietnam. The Vietnamese contend that since the Shanghai communiqué of 1972, China had been following a pro-West policy that could have jeopardized the socialist development strategies of Vietnam in the South, which included a reorganization of Chinese economic interests in Vietnam.[34]

In addition to the usual assertions made by China against Hanoi, the ASEAN states accused Vietnam of instigating the exodus of refugees for several purposes:

1. To create social, economic, and military hardships in neighboring countries.

2. To take money from refugees as Vietnam allows and encourages refugees to leave as long as they pay exorbitant fees to boost the country's treasury.

3. The Soviet Union encouraged the exodus in an effort to increase hegemony in the region. (The ASEAN states initially believed Moscow benefited from the hardships the refugee crisis created in Southeast Asia by weakening the nations' abilities to deal with the crisis. China repeatedly supported such assertions and argued that the exodus was also partially the Soviets' fault.)[35]

But the situation for ethnic Chinese living in Vietnam since 1979 changed somewhat. The arguments of mistreatment gradually died down, and the focus of the Sino-Vietnamese conflict shifted to issues surrounding Vietnamese involvement in Cambodia and Soviet involvement in Indochina. This is evident by considering events affecting the ethnic Chinese from 1979 to the present.

The Ethnic Chinese Problem Since 1979

The dispute over Chinese living in Vietnam has been described by some as a dead issue.[36] This statement is perhaps an exaggeration, but it does indicate how quickly the problem went from an item of major importance to a seldom-mentioned dispute of the past. There are four major possibilities that need to be noted in order to understand why the problem of Chinese living in Vietnam is not nearly as heated now as it was in the past.

By the end of 1980, refugees from Vietnam who returned to China numbered about 260,000. At the end of the same year, about one million "boat people" had left Vietnam, of which 70 percent are estimated to have been of Chinese descent.[37] The exodus of such a large number of Chinese residents constitutes a major change in the situation for Chinese living in Vietnam. It is assumed that many of those who fled Vietnam were in fact those who previously had played important roles in the Vietnamese economy. This leaves those Chinese behind who perhaps had less to lose from the Vietnamese reforms or who perhaps felt that leaving was a greater risk than staying in Vietnam. It is also possible that many ethnic Chinese considered themselves more Vietnamese than Chinese and chose to remain in Vietnam. At any rate, the number of Chinese living in Vietnam in 1982 was significantly reduced from 1978. Chinese living in Vietnam would therefore not be considered to be nearly the problem for Hanoi as it was in the past.

A second reason why the issue has gradually faded resulted from a change in Vietnam's attitude toward economic development. By 1982 it became obvious that the various economic plans instituted in the late 1970s were not effective in bringing about the desired economic results. The effect was a limited acceptance of capitalism that revived the influence of Chinese still living in Cholon. Small markets once again surfaced, making products available that were in years past condemned by the government. Chinese networks that were thought to have been destroyed during the turmoil of 1978–1980 resurfaced. The economic successes of these bangs once again began reversing some of the government-sponsored campaigns to transform the economy.[38] With the huge dependence Vietnam has on the Soviet Union for economic assistance, plus the added hardships resulting from Vietnamese war efforts in Cambodia, any income-producing activity is considered a boon to the overall economy.

The major reason that the overseas Chinese represented less of a problem was that the other issues in the Sino-Vietnamese dispute took center stage. As the negotiations following the war in 1979 began, it was obvious that Cambodia and overall competition for influence in Indochina and Southeast Asia in general were the main problems dividing Vietnam and China. Even issues like the presence of the Soviet Union in Indochina, the border/territorial dispute, and relations with other regional and world powers took on more importance to Hanoi and Beijing than did the ethnic Chinese problem.

China welcomed the drop-off in refugee numbers as it had limited resources to settle refugees returning to China. Beijing therefore probably watched the situation very closely to insure that another large-scale exodus did not begin anew. At the same time, Hanoi did not want to risk a second war with China and, with the relative absence of the overseas Chinese problem, the chances of war were at least modestly reduced.

The final reason why the issue declined in importance resulted from efforts on Hanoi's part. As mentioned above, Hanoi received very little sympathy from the international community during the refugee crisis. The ASEAN states were direct in their attack against Vietnam for inciting the refugee exodus. Japan, the United States, other Western nations, and the United Nations High Command on Refugees sorely condemned Vietnam during the exodus period. Vietnam determined that it was in its best interest to foster better relations with the major powers of the world and realized that a reoccurrence of the refugee crisis could only damage hopes for forging new relations.

All in all, attention to other matters enabled China and Vietnam, if not to remove, at least temporarily to ignore the tragedy of the overseas Chinese in Vietnam.

Conclusion

The purpose of this chapter has been to cover the major aspects of the ethnic Chinese problem in the Sino-Vietnamese conflict. It was first pointed out that there has always been an adversarial relationship between Chinese residents in Vietnam and the Vietnamese government. This was especially so in the past two decades, as the government of the Socialist Republic of Vietnam sought to reorganize the country's economic structure, which meant disbanding considerable Chinese influence, particularly in the South. As a result of these policies, also considering the overall decline of Sino-Vietnamese relations generally in the post-1975 era, violence and widespread disarray followed, leading to an enormous exodus of Chinese out of Vietnam.

A second major aspect covered in this chapter suggests the diplomatic tussle that accompanied the refugee exodus showed that the issue of Chinese living in Vietnam was aggravated by a rapid decline in relations between Vietnam and China generally. As the official pronouncements came out of Hanoi and Beijing, it became clear that Chinese residents in Vietnam had indeed presented the Vietnamese government and people with a hardship that was difficult to handle. It also indicated that China was using the issue as a mask to hide pressing issues, such as the increase in Vietnamese influence in Cambodia, and other aspects of the Sino-Vietnamese contest. When diplomacy failed to stop the Chinese exodus from Vietnam, this was seen as just one justification of many for China to launch a punitive invasion of Vietnam in February 1979.

Finally, the issue of Chinese living in Vietnam has, for the time being, become less important in recent years. The reduced Chinese population living in Vietnam, Hanoi's desire for improved economic conditions and relations abroad, and a general focus on other issues in the Sino-Vietnamese contest have diverted attention from the ethnic Chinese issue.

There is no discounting the fact, however, that the overseas Chinese issue caused significant problems between Vietnam and

China in the past, particularly in 1978 and 1979. It is difficult to assess how much the Chinese government was concerned about the mistreatment of Chinese living in Vietnam. Some Chinese accounts may have exaggerated China's humanitarian concern.[39] Vietnam, too, has been guilty of exploiting the issue to vent its frustrations from other areas of disagreement with the Chinese.

Herein lies the tragedy. Everywhere the refugees fled after leaving Vietnam, they were not welcomed by host nations. The crisis could probably have been less drastic if other issues surrounding Vietnamese-Chinese relations had not been so serious. Probably half of the one million who fled Vietnam by boat died on the South China Sea, and those who made it to China or other nations found only reluctant acceptance.

When considered in terms of human life, the refugee crisis constitutes the most serious aspect of the Sino-Vietnamese conflict. Far more people died from this aspect of the conflict than from the actual wars started in 1978 and 1979. The only way human lives could have been saved was for Beijing and Hanoi to seek ways to prevent the tragedy from occurring, as both are responsible for what happened. But this was dependent on a willingness to solve problems through diplomacy and possibly with the cooperation of other nation-states.

There is more than a remote chance that further problems will arise from Chinese living in Vietnam. It could prove serious if there is a total breakdown in relations between Vietnam and China, leading to problems similar to those of the late 1970s. In a worst case scenario, an all-out war between the two nations could lead to another crisis for the Chinese in Vietnam. Preferably, both Hanoi and Beijing have determined that the costs of the refugee crisis and the war of 1979 make both of these possibilities unthinkable. The final conclusion of this aspect of the Sino-Vietnamese conflict is therefore largely dependent on the other issues separating the two countries.

7

Conclusion

Dragons Entangled: A Region at War

This study has attempted to provide a broad understanding of Sino-Vietnamese relations by looking at both the major sources of conflict and the irritants that accentuate tensions between the two countries. At this point it is appropriate to review briefly the factors that have contributed to this conflict.

Major Sources of Conflict

Historical Animosity

This study began by looking at the historical rift that has separated China and Vietnam. The two countries had dealings with each other as early as 700 B.C., and China made Vietnam a tributary state around 200 B.C. The Vietnamese have continually sought to keep their identity and territory independent of Chinese control since the time of tributary status. They were most successful in accomplishing this goal when China's various dynastic regimes were in general disarray and losing their ability to rule effectively.

During the last century, the Vietnamese viewed China in

mixed terms. China was considered a helper when Vietnam was fighting for its independence from the West, mostly because it was also in China's interest to establish a buffer against non-Asian powers. But China was considered by many Vietnamese nationalists to be too involved in the direction and scope of Vietnam's fight for independence. This factor still figures prominently in today's conflict.

Conflict over Indochina

Even before the Vietnam war ended in 1975, Hanoi and Beijing were already suspicious of each other's role in the affairs of the other Indochinese states—particularly Cambodia. The Chinese attacked Vietnam following Vietnam's December 1978 invasion of Cambodia and Hanoi's failure to take Beijing's persistent diplomatic and military threats seriously. After the initial war between Vietnam and China ended in March 1979, China continued every effort to reverse the Vietnamese presence in Cambodia, fearing Vietnam was very near to realizing a Hanoi-dominated Indochina and thus completely encircling China's southern borders.

The Sino-Vietnamese conflict has tremendous implications for the two nations in terms of regional and international power. Hanoi desperately feels an Indochina alliance lends security to Vietnam vis-à-vis its assertive neighbor China, and also believes the alliance gives Vietnam added clout in the region and in the international community. China views the alliance as not just a threat from its neighbor Vietnam, but from the Soviet Union as well, which has supported the Vietnamese in its efforts in Cambodia.

The Superpowers, ASEAN, and Cambodia

The Soviet friendship with Hanoi has been a source of discontent in Beijing for a long time. When Vietnam stepped up relations with Moscow following the U.S. defeat in Indochina, Beijing immediately sought ways to check combined Soviet-Vietnamese power. This was partially accomplished by improving relations with Japan, the United States, and the ASEAN nations. Though Vietnam was considered the immediate threat, the USSR remained China's archenemy in the international community.

Hanoi is not overly excited about its relationship with Moscow and has tried to lessen Soviet influence in the region. But at the same time, Vietnam remains heavily dependent on the Soviet Union as its primary source of development aid which has run in the billions of dollars. Until recently, Hanoi saw a close relationship with Moscow as necessary for maintaining a Hanoi-dominated Indochina alliance.

Hanoi has failed to obtain Washington's recognition primarily because of Hanoi's invasion of Cambodia, its close relationship with Moscow, and what Washington perceives as Hanoi's unwillingness to resolve the MIA-POW issue.

Like the Vietnamese, China sought normalized relations with the United States to increase China's importance as a regional and international power, to open up trade opportunities to the outside world, and to check Soviet influence in Asia. The Chinese were successful in winning U.S. recognition. Normalization has boosted both Beijing and Washington's influence in the East Asian region.

ASEAN has continuously sought a Cambodian settlement. As the Jakarta Informal Meetings neared, ASEAN began to fear a resurgence of Khmer Rouge power and thus shifted much of its concern about Vietnamese domination to the unpredictable nature of the CGDK alliance. The fate of the KR continues to be the main stumbling block in the conflict to this day.

Irritants in the Sino-Vietnamese Conflict

The Border/Territorial Conflict

China's invasion of Vietnam in February 1979 was justified by Beijing as an attempt to teach Vietnam a lesson and to reclaim

Chinese territory which Vietnam was supposedly occupying illegally. Though several territories are disputed by China and Vietnam, the principal reason for invading Vietnam was to punish and warn Vietnam for its activities in Cambodia. Thus the territorial/border dispute serves as an irritant and not as a principal cause of disagreement. This is further evident from the fact that Vietnam and China frequently clash along their common border when Vietnam begins a new offensive against CGDK elements inside Cambodia, or when China feels military conflict will help bring regional and international pressure on Vietnam to relinquish its goals in Cambodia.

The Ethnic Chinese in Vietnam

Like the border/territorial disputes, the ethnic Chinese living in Vietnam also complicate the larger issue of competition for influence in Indochina. The mass exodus of ethnic Chinese out of Vietnam from 1978 to 1980 indicates the severity of competition between the two countries and does not constitute the major point of discord by itself. In short, the presence of ethnic Chinese in Vietnam becomes a serious challenge to Hanoi only when relations between Hanoi and Beijing are seriously strained, as they have been for the past decade and a half.

Some General Conclusions of this Study

The principal conclusion that can be drawn from this study is that the Sino-Vietnamese conflict, like so many other major conflicts in the world today, is primarily born out of the struggle for regional influence and security. If Vietnam and China were not neighbors, and thus not seeking to dominate the same region at the expense of the other, it is probable they would get along very well, considering their common struggle against Western influence and their shared historical views of revolution. But their existence as neighbors seeking to increase their long-term security and influence puts them directly at odds with one another.

This may be accentuated by the fact that both China and Vietnam are relative newcomers to the modern nation-state system and are both seeking power and prestige in the international community, which in part depends on success in realizing their respective goals in Indochina.

Like the Sino-Soviet conflict, the China-Vietnam dispute has very little to do with ideology. Marxist ideology is seldom referred to by either Hanoi or Beijing in their rhetoric concerning the conflict. Though specific policies are often attacked by both countries, they are not grounded in any particular notions of Marxism. Instead, the two countries routinely accuse each other of being hegemonist in nature by seeking to gain an unfair advantage over the peoples and countries of Indochina.

Regime changes in Vietnam and China affect the degree of cooperation and conflict between Hanoi and Beijing, but do not change the fundamental issues that divide them. This has been evident in the transition from the Maoists to the Deng Xiaoping group in China, and from the Pham Van Dong–Le Duan group to a coalition of younger Vietnamese currently seeking top positions of power. The intensity of the conflict is sometimes immediately influenced by shifts in policy or in the initiation of new policies during a regime change, but long-term objectives remain unchanged.

The two superpowers are careful not to alter the stalemate in Indochina in such a way that would destabilize the Southeast Asian region generally. For this reason, the United States has been reluctant to step up its role in the conflict beyond what it has been since 1979. The Soviet Union has opted to decrease gradually its financial and military commitment to Vietnam's Cambodia operation. China has recognized this attitude in Moscow and has sought improved relations with the Soviet Union, despite continued Soviet involvement in the region.

East Asian nation-states have adjusted to the conflict and view it as a long-term struggle that has no immediate answers. Japan has proceeded with development loans and projects in both Vietnam and China, even in waters considered disputed, with relative ease and without the immediate threat of reprisal by either Beijing or Hanoi. The ASEAN states continue to seek a solution to the Cambodian conflict in order to stabilize Cambodia and quell the Sino-Vietnamese conflict. In part, this resulted in the Jakarta Informal Meeting of July 1988 and subsequent meetings that have raised hopes that a settlement will be forthcoming.

What Does the Future Hold?

It is unlikely that the Sino-Vietnamese conflict will be resolved in the immediate future. Both Hanoi and Beijing feel bound to support their policies in Indochina for practical considerations. Neither China nor Vietnam trusts each other's intentions in Indochina. Total abandonment of policies where much blood and effort has been spent is perceived as too great a concession for either Vietnam or China to consider.

But the conflict is changing rapidly. Recent momentum on the part of all parties involved to reach a viable solution has led to new hopes of solving the Cambodian crisis and, to a degree, patching up the Sino-Vietnamese relationship. But it remains crucial to consider the long- and short-term goals of the Beijing and Hanoi leaderships. Many argue a settlement of the Cambodian conflict and Sino-Vietnamese conflict is prevented by Beijing's willingness to support the Khmer Rouge and failure to throw its full support behind the on-again off-again negotiation process.

But even if China were to demonstrate its acceptance of the talk process and agree to cease supporting the KR, there are no guarantees that the Khmer Rouge would go along with Beijing, and it is not likely that a peace would be negotiated to the liking of all parties involved. Cambodia will remain unstable for some time, even after a settlement has been agreed to, as the different factions seek ways to maintain a position of power in a new government. This will directly interest Beijing and Hanoi just as it has in the past and will continue the likelihood of conflict between the two Asian powers. Hopefully it will not be as volatile a conflict as it has been in the past.

Notes

Introduction

1. This is a conservative figure based on newspaper estimates of border deaths, deaths at sea, and war victims. It does not include an accounting of those killed in Cambodia, or those of have died since 1982.

Chapter 1

1. There are many examples of China's plea to normalize relations in accordance with the traditional friendship between the two nations. Though they are not explicit on the exact nature of this friendship, it is assumed that Beijing is referring more to relations since the founding of the People's Republic in 1949. See *Speech Made by Han Nianlong, Head of the Chinese Government Delegation and Vice Minister for Foreign Affairs, at the Sixth Plenary Meeting of the Sino-Vietnamese Negotiations on 28 June 1979* (UN Proceedings of the General Assembly, 34th Session).

2. Ministry of Foreign Affairs, Socialist Republic of Vietnam, *The Truth About Vietnam-China Relations Over the Last 30 Years* (Hanoi: October 1979). Reprinted in *Chinese Law and Government* 16, 1 (Spring 1983).

3. Vietnam at this time was comprised of the major river valleys which currently lie in the Tonkin area or present-day North Vietnam.

4. The Chinese name for Vietnam adopted at this time (Yue Nan) literally mean "southern barbarians." The Chinese characters and pronunciation has remained the same to the present day. See Keith Weller Taylor, *The Birth of Vietnam* (Berkeley: University of California Press, 1983), p. 78.

5. Mark Mancall, "The Ch'ing Tribute System: An Interpretive Essay," in *The Chinese World Order*, ed. John K. Fairbank (Cambridge: Harvard University Press, 1968), pp. 66–67.

6. Taylor, *The Birth of Vietnam*, p. 28.

7. From P.J. Honey, *Genesis of a Tragedy: The Historical Background to the Vietnam War* (London: Ernest Benn, 1968), p. 2.

8. Taylor, *The Birth of Vietnam*, p. 33.

9. Ibid., pp. 40–41.

10. Ibid., p. 334.

11. Alexander Barton Woodside, *Vietnam and the Chinese Model* (Cambridge: Harvard University Press, 1971), pp. 12–14. Woodside suggests the Vietnamese did not necessarily look upon the Chinese as a colonial power but as a group who, through excessive force, had "lost the hearts of the people." See p. 21.

12. Taylor, *The Birth of Vietnam,* p. 53.

13. Ibid., pp. 126–31.

14. Ibid., p. 249.

15. See Taylor, *The Birth of Vietnam,* pp. 190–210, for a more detailed explanation of the decline of the Tang and the rise of Vietnam.

16. Albert M. Craig, John K. Fairbank, and Edwin O. Reischauer, *East Asia: Tradition and Transformation* (Boston: Houghton Mifflin, 1973), p. 262.

17. Joseph Buttinger, *A Dragon Defiant: A Short History of Vietnam* (New York: Praeger, 1972), p. 39.

18. Ibid., p. 42.

19. Ibid., p. 45.

20. Helen B. Lamb, *Vietnam's Will to Live* (New York: Monthly Review Press, 1972), p. 29.

21. Craig, Fairbank, and Reischauer, *East Asia,* p. 268.

22. Ibid., pp. 273–74.

23. Buttinger, *A Dragon Defiant,* p. 49.

24. See Lam Truong Buu, "Intervention Versus Tribute in Sino-Vietnamese Relations, 1788–1790," in *The Chinese World Order,* ed. Fairbank, p. 165. Lam argues it was in the interest of both the Chinese and the Vietnamese to carry on the tribute system so that China felt secure and to keep the Chinese from directly intervening in the affairs of the Nguyen government.

25. Fairbank, ed., *The Chinese World Order,* pp. 10–11.

26. Ibid., p. 13.

27. Woodside, *Vietnam and the Chinese Model,* pp. 24–28.

28. Buttinger, *A Dragon Defiant,* p. 56.

29. Craig, Fairbank, and Reischauer, *East Asia,* p. 275.

30. Buttinger, *A Dragon Defiant,* p. 69.

31. Lamb, *Vietnam's Will to Live,* pp. 135–36.

32. Ibid., p. 227.

33. King C. Chen, *Vietnam and China, 1938–1954* (Princeton: Princeton University Press, 1969), p. 10.

34. See Henry McAleavy, *Black Flags in Vietnam: The Story of a Chinese Intervention* (New York: Macmillan, 1968). McAleavy's book has an excellent discussion of China's fears of being surrounded by colonial powers.

35. J.F. Cairns, *The Eagle and the Lotus: Western Intervention in Vietnam, 1847–1971* (Melbourne: Lansdome Press, 1979), p. 11.

36. Chen, *Vietnam and China,* p. 16.

37. Jean Sainteny, *Ho Chi Minh and His Vietnam: A Personal Memoir* (Chicago: Cowles Book, 1972), p. 34.

38. Ibid., pp. 34–35.

39. Chen, *Vietnam and China,* p. 18.

40. Ibid., p. 41.

41. Ibid., pp. 84–93.

42. Sainteny, *Ho Chi Minh and His Vietnam,* p. 48.

43. McAleavy, *Black Flags in Vietnam,* pp. 285–86.

44. Sainteny, *Ho Chi Minh and His Vietnam,* p. 119.

45. Chen, *Vietnam and China,* pp. 118–21.

46. Ibid., p. 145.

47. Buttinger, *A Dragon Defiant,* pp. 90–91.

48. Chen, *Vietnam and China,* pp. 274–78.

49. Ibid., p. 310.

50. Stanley Karnow, *Vietnam: A History* (New York: Penguin, 1984), p. 192.

51. Buttinger, *A Dragon Defiant,* pp. 91–92.

52. Karnow, *Vietnam,* p. 193.

53. Ibid., p. 328.

54. Ibid., p. 200.

55. See Dwight D. Eisenhower, *Mandate for Change: 1953–56* (New York: Doubleday and Company, 1963), pp. 332–75. It is argued by some that the United States' hesitation to support the accord may have doomed the political settlement as covered by the agreement, which called for a nationwide election to be monitored and administered by neutral nations. The American commitment to the conflict in Vietnam was already costing Washington dearly. By 1954 the United States had spent $2.5 billion against the Vietnamese, in the form of assistance to the French—more than France received in Marshall Aid funds.

56. Karnow, *Vietnam,* p. 204.

57. Ibid., p. 224.

58. See Karnow, *Vietnam,* p. 377, for a discussion of the intricacies and background of the Tonkin incident and the gradual commitment of the United States toward direct intervention in the war in Vietnam.

59. As pointed out by Eugene K. Lawson, *The Sino-Vietnamese Conflict* (New York: Praeger, 1984), this was a major reason for the DRV-PRC split.

60. Karnow, *Vietnam,* pp. 452–53.

61. Ibid., p. 411.

62. See Richard M. Nixon, *The Memoirs of Richard Nixon* (New York: Grosset and Dunlap, 1978), p. 344. It is clear that Nixon's view of bringing a speedy end to the war was in fact completely in harmony with the efforts of presidents Johnson, Kennedy, and Eisenhower.

63. Henry A. Kissinger, *The White House Years* (Boston: Little, Brown, 1979), p. 695.

64. Immanuel C.Y. Hsu, *The Rise of Modern China* (New York: Oxford University Press, 1986), pp. 107–19.

65. Ibid., pp. 401–4, 465.

66. Thomas W. Robinson, "The Sino-Soviet Border Dispute: Background Development, and the March 1969 Clashes," *American Political Science Review* 66 (December 1972): 1176–79.

67. Ibid., p. 1201.

68. David McLellan, *Marxism After Marx* (Boston: Houghton Mifflin, 1979), pp. 234–37. Also see Wolfgang Leonhard, *Three Faces of Marxism: The Political Concepts of Soviet Ideology, Maoism, and Humanist Marxism* (New York: Paragon Books, 1979), pp. 227–32, 242–45, 255–57.

69. See Karnow, *Vietnam,* pp. 580–85 for a good discussion of the costs of the Vietnam war to Beijing and Moscow.

70. Kissinger, *The White House Years,* pp. 173–86.

71. Ibid., pp. 191–92.

72. It is argued by most analysts that North Vietnamese goals in the war were clear by 1970. The Vietnamese had no intention of allowing Beijing or Moscow to tell them when to stop their war; nor would they stop until they had a Vietnamese stronghold throughout all of Indochina. These intentions were probably one of the major reasons for the United States to continue its effort in Vietnam. The Chinese were displeased as well and tried different channels to discourage the Vietnamese from following through with their efforts. The Soviets were not firm on the situation, only fearing that continued conflict would sour detente and seriously damage the prospects for a new peace with the West.

73. Kissinger, *The White House Years,* p. 1113.

74. Nixon, *Memoirs,* p. 706. In later attempts Nixon turned both to Beijing and Moscow to pressure the Vietnamese to sit down and discuss terms for ending the war. See also p. 730 and p. 742.

75. Henry A. Kissinger, *Years of Upheaval* (Boston: Little, Brown, 1982).

76. Karnow, *Vietnam,* p. 646.

77. Troung Nhu Tang, *A Vietcong Memoir* (New York: Harcourt, Brace Jovanovich, 1985), pp. 255–57.

78. Karnow, *Vietnam,* pp. 31–32.

Chapter 2

1. *Washington Post,* May 1, 1975.

2. Under the terms of the Paris agreements, the Provisional Revolutionary Government was supposed to handle the day-to-day affairs of South Vietnam until an acceptable agreement could be made on the future of Vietnam by the Saigon and Hanoi authorities. The plan was never popular among Hanoi's leaders because it meant the continuation of a two-Vietnam policy. China continued to use the PRG organization to carry on some official business with South Vietnam, a situation that made Hanoi angry. (See chapter 1.)

3. U.S. State Department document, "Da Nang Incident: June 1975," found in the University of California, Berkeley, Indochina Archives, Vietnam Collection (hereafter referred to as DRV Indochina Files), June 1975.

4. *New York Times,* August 15, 1975.

5. "Statement of Chinese Foreign Ministry on Expulsion of Chinese Residents by Viet Nam," Ministry of Foreign Affairs, People's Republic of China,

June 9, 1978. Reprinted in the *Beijing Review,* June 16, 1978, pp. 13–17.

6. U.S. State Department memo, February 19–26, 1976, "Indications of Strained Relations Between China and Vietnam," DRV Indochina Files, February 1976.

7. U.S. State Department memo, April 12, 1976, DRV Indochina Files. Most memos in this file do not have a title. The DEV files are from 1967 to present day. An ongoing project at the University of California, Berkeley.

8. Richard Wich, *Sino-Soviet Crisis Politics: A Study Of Political Change and Communication* (Cambridge: Council on East Asian Studies, 1980), pp. 2–5.

9. *New York Times,* July 11, 1975.

10. *Far Eastern Economic Review* (hereafter *FEER*), June 11, 1976.

11. In particular, Sun mentioned the U.S. military presence in Southeast Asia was generally acceptable to China but not Vietnam. See U.S. State Department memo, "SRV-PRC Relations: July 1976," DRV Indochina Files, July 1976.

12. See "PRC's Emerging Policy in Southeast Asia," DRV Indochina Files, December 1976.

13. Pao-min Chang, *Beijing, Hanoi, and the Overseas Chinese* (Berkeley: University of California Press, 1982), pp. 21, 25. Immediately prior to the purge, the Vietnamese Workers Party (the official name of Vietnam's communist party) held a convention which the Chinese declined to attend. No reasons were given, though the Chinese did send a congratulatory note. See Kyodo News Service, FBIS *Daily Report, China,* December 10, 1976.

14. *FEER,* March 12, 1976.

15. New China News Agency (hereafter NCNA), July 3, 1976, FBIS *Daily Report, China,* July 4, 1976.

16. NCNA, FBIS *Daily Report, China* December 17, 1976.

17. The text of the memorandum was reprinted in the *Beijing Review,* March 20, 1979, pp. 17–22.

18. Craig Etcheson, *The Rise and Demise of Democratic Kampuchea,* (Boulder: Westview Press, 1984), p. 16.

19. Finnish Inquiry Commission, *Kampuchea: Decade of the Genocide,* Edited by Kimmo Kiljunen, (London: Zed Books, 1984).

20. Karl D. Jackson, "Cambodia 1977: Gone to Pot," *Asian Survey* (January 1978): 79–80.

21. C.L. Chou, "China's Policy Towards Laos: Politics of Neutralization," in *Contemporary Laos: Studies in Politics and Society of the Lao People's Democratic Republic,* ed. Martin Stuart-Fox (New York: St. Martin's Press, 1982), p. 298.

22. Carlyle A. Thayer, "Laos and Vietnam: The Anatomy of Special Relationship," in *Contemporary Laos,* ed. Stuart-Fox, pp. 255–56.

23. Arthur J. Dommen, *Laos: Keystone of Indochina* (Boulder: Westview Press, 1985), pp. 125–26.

24. Chou, "China's Policy Towards Laos," p. 298.

25. "Treaty of Friendship and Cooperation Between the Lao People's Republic and the Socialist Republic of Vietnam," July 18, 1977. Reprinted in *Chinese Law and Government* 16, 1 (Spring 1983).

26. *Asia Yearbook, 1976* (Hong Kong: Far Eastern Economic Review, 1976).

27. *FEER,* October 14, 1977, p. 30.

28. *FEER,* September 23, 1977, p. 30.

29. *Vietnam Courier* (November 1977): 7–9.

30. "More on Hanoi's White Book," *Beijing Review,* November 30, 1979, pp. 11–15.

31. "Comrade Hua Kuo-feng's Speech," *Beijing Review,* November 23, 1977.

32. "Comrade Le Duan's Speech," *Beijing Review,* November 23, 1977.

33. NCNA, December 30, 1977, FBIS *Daily Report, China,* December 31, 1977.

34. AFP, FBIS *Daily Report, East Asia,* December 31, 1977.

35. *FEER,* January 13, 1978, pp. 10–11.

36. *FEER,* February 3, 1978, p. 22.

37. Some analysts believe Cambodia reacted too quickly to the Vietnamese threats by attacking Vietnamese villages. This, it is argued, blew the conflict into the open. See Karl D. Jackson, "Cambodia 1978: War, Pillage, and Purge in Democratic Kampuchea" *Asian Survey,* (January 1979).

38. See Etcheson *The Rise and Demise of Democratic Kampuchea,* pp. 86–89, 193–97.

39. Vietnam News Agency (VNA), FBIS *Daily Report, East Asia,* July 7, 1978.

40. Socialist Republic of Vietnam, Ministry of Foreign Affairs, "Report on the International Strategy of China," June 1978, DRV Indochina Files, June 1980.

41. U.S. State Department memo, DRV Indochina Files, June 1978.

42. TASS, July 3, 1978, FBIS *Daily Report, East Asia,* July 6, 1978.

43. *Christian Science Monitor,* September 29, 1978.

44. U.S. State Department memo, DRV Indochina Files, September 1978.

45. *Renmin ribao,* September 26, 1978, FBIS *Daily Report, China,* September 26, 1978.

46. "Treaty of Friendship and Cooperation Between the Socialist Republic of Vietnam and the Union of Soviet Socialist Republics," November 3, 1978. Reprinted in *Chinese Law and Government* 16, 1 (Spring 1983).

47. Deng Xiaoping's news conference in Bangkok, "Vietnam-Soviet Treaty Threatens World Peace and Security." Reprinted in *Beijing Review,* November 17, 1978.

48. U.S. State Department memo, DRV Indochina File, January 1979.

49. Notes, DRV Indochina Files, January 1979.

50. "Statement by Chinese Foreign Ministry Spokesman Supporting Kampuchea's Just Stand and Condemning Vietnamese Authorities' Aggression and Subversion," *Beijing Review,* December 22, 1978.

51. U.S. State Department memo, DRV Indochina Files, December 1978.

52. U.S. Department of State, Foreign Ministry of the People's Republic of China, "Joint Communiqué on the Establishment of Diplomatic Relations Between the United States of America and the People's Republic of China, January 1, 1979," *State Department Bulletin* 79 (January 1979): 25.

53. "Chairman Hua Gives Press Conference," *Beijing Review,* December 22, 1978, pp. 9–11.

54. Despite claims that the Sino-U.S. rapproachment did not surprise the SRV, outside observers stated that the move shocked the Vietnamese, who felt they had lost the "normalization game." Hanoi-watchers argued Vietnam tried to win the friendship of an old enemy (the United States), but was forced into an unhappy alliance with the Soviet Union. See *FEER,* December 29, 1978, pp. 14–15.

55. Internal U.S. State Department document, DRV Indochina Files, December 1978.

56. "Chinese Government Statement, January 14, 1979," *Beijing Review,* January 19, 1979.

57. VNA, February 10, 1979, FBIS *Daily Report, East Asia,* February 11, 1979.

58. *New York Times,* February 18, 1979. It is important to note that the March 2, 1979, issue of the *Beijing Review* said China's invasion of Vietnam was a response to Vietnamese aggression on China's border since August 10, 1978, the ill-treatment of ethnic Chinese living in Vietnam and subsequent exile of Chinese residents, and the armed attack on Chinese fishing vessels by Vietnam in international waters.

59. *New York Times,* February 18, 1979. The *New York Times* also reported on March 6, 1979, that China denied Vietnam's incursion into Cambodia had anything to do with the Chinese punitive strike against Vietnam.

60. TASS, February 18, 1979, reported in the *New York Times,* February 19, 1979.

61. *Christian Science Monitor,* February 20, 1979.

62. VNA, February 24, 1979, FBIS Daily Report, East Asia, February 26, 1979.

63. *FEER,* March 2, 1979, p. 12.

64. Outside observers speculate that by February 25 the Chinese were low on supplies and manpower. To continue the large-scale operation would require more divisions and support units than Beijing felt they could deploy. See the *New York Times,* February 26, 1979.

65. *New York Times,* February 28, 1979.

66. NCNA, reported by *Washington Post* and *New York Times,* March 6, 1979.

67. *New York Times,* March 6, 1979.

68. From an AFP release by Jean Thoraval and reprinted in the *New York Times* on March 27, 1979.

69. *Beijing Review,* March 23, 1979.

Chapter 3

1. U.S. State Department memo, DRV Indochina Files, September 1979.

2. "Foreign Affairs Trends," secret PRC document translated by the U.S. Department of State, DRV Indochina Files, September 1979.

3. *Beijing Review,* March 23, 1979, pp. 21–23.

4. Ibid., pp. 22–23.

5. VNA, FBIS *Daily Report, East Asia,* April 19, 1979.

6. Hanoi Domestic Service, April 18, 1979, FBIS *Daily Report, East Asia,* March 21, 1980.

7. "Speech by Han Nianlong at Second Round of Sino-Vietnamese Talks in Hanoi," April 26, 1979. See *Beijing Review,* May 4, 1979, p. 16.

8. AFP, Hong Kong, FBIS *Daily Report, East Asia,* May 4, 1979.

9. See United Nations documents A/34/341, S/13420 and A/34/351, S/23434 for the opening statements of the vice-ministers of the People's Republic of China and the Socialist Republic of Vietnam, June 28, 1979.

10. China's pledge for "teaching Vietnam a second lesson" actually began shortly after the end of the war in March, but as talks stalled, many believed China would act on her threats.

11. The document was released by the SRV's Ministry of Foreign Affairs. It is reprinted in *Chinese Law and Government* 16, 1 (Spring 1983).

12. "On Hanoi's White Book," *Beijing Review,* November 23, 1979.

13. Ibid., p. 8.

14. *FEER,* May 30, 1980, pp. 17–18.

15. *Vietnam Courier* (October 1980) and (December 1980– April 1981).

16. *FEER,* November 28, 1980, pp. 12–13.

17. U.S. State Department memo, DRV Indochina Files, April 1980.

18. U.S. State Department summary, October 1980, DRV Indochina Files, October 1980.

19. *FEER,* November 28, 1980, pp. 12–13.

20. See Pao-min Chang, "Beijing Versus Hanoi," *Asian Survey* (May 1983): 604.

21. Ibid., p. 607.

22. China put enormous pressure on ASEAN to ensure that talks with Vietnam about Indochina's future did not proceed without the Chinese being involved in the proceedings. See "The Kampuchean Issue: Its Origin and Major Aspects," *Beijing Review,* September 12, 1983.

23. On two occasions, in particular, the Chinese felt that Thailand was softening its approach to Hanoi. This resulted in border fighting that Beijing said reflected Vietnam's intentions in Indochina. See *FEER,* May 5, 1983, pp. 42–43, and June 16, 1983, pp. 12–14. See also "Frontier Artillery Fire in Retaliation," *Beijing Review,* April 19, 1984, p. 11.

24. *Beijing Review,* September 12, 1983.

25. *FEER,* February 18, 1981, and May 8, 1981.

26. *Beijing Review,* December 6, 1982.

27. *FEER,* January 24, 1984.

28. U.S. State Department memo, "USSR-SRV Economic Relations: November 1980," DRV Indochina Files, November 1980.

29. The Chinese estimate that SRV military expenses accounted for 41.4 percent of that country's GNP in 1977, 40.4 percent in 1978, and 47 percent in 1979. NCNA, November 29, 1980, FBIS *Daily Report, China,* November 30, 1980.

30. PRC foreign ministry memo, July 13, 1981, NCNA, FBIS *Daily Report, China,* July 14, 1981.

31. See, for example, the "Foreign Ministry Statement, March 1, 1983," *Beijing Review,* March 7, 1983, and *Beijing Review,* January 9, 1984. Beijing attempted to use international law to build a case to show the illegal activities of the Soviet Union in Asia in order to maintain a general feeling of anti-Soviet support in the region.

32. In a Hanoi radio broadcast in April 1985, for example, no mention was made of the Soviet Union in any of Vietnam's conflicts involving the United States, China, or the Khmer Rouge. See FBIS *Daily Report, East Asia,* May 8, 1985.

33. *Los Angeles Times,* October 5, 1986.

34. *China Daily,* December 1, 1987.

35. "Chronology of U.S./SRV POW-MIA Activities, May 1981–July 1984," DRV Indochina Files.

36. Ibid., p. 4.

37. Nearly all of Vietnam's official news releases on the Sino-Vietnamese conflict mention that China, the United States, and ASEAN have engaged in a campaign to isolate Vietnam in the international community, by lying about Vietnamese abuses in Indochina. See, for example, UN document A/34/351, S/13434, June 28, 1979, and also Hanoi's white book on Sino-Vietnamese relations.

38. For a fuller discussion on the UN's condemnation and dealings with Vietnam, see Chang, "Beijing Versus Hanoi," p. 602.

39. *FEER,* May 26, 1983, pp. 14–16.

40. *Beijing Review,* October 1, 1984.

41. *Beijing Review,* February 20, 1984, p. 9.

42. *FEER,* June 14, 1984, pp. 29–30.

43. *FEER,* February 7, 1985, pp. 10–11.

44. *FEER,* May 30, 1985, pp. 15–16.

45. *FEER,* March 28, 1985, pp. 10–11.

46. *Christian Science Monitor,* April 10, 1985.

47. *Beijing Review,* March 25, 1986.

48. *Beijing Review,* October 12, 1981, p. 15. See also *Christian Science Monitor,* January 16, 1986, p. 10.

49. *FEER,* April 10, 1986, pp. 35–36.

50. *FEER,* August 14, 1986, pp. 37–38.

51. Moscow Television Service, July 28, 1986, FBIS *Daily Report, Soviet Union,* July 29, 1986.

52. *Indochina Chronology* (July–September 1986) mentions that only delegates from Laos, Kampuchea, and the Soviet Union attended Le Duan's funeral—a curious response from the communist world, considering he was head of the VCP and his importance in Vietnamese affairs.

53. *FEER,* August 7, 1986, pp. 28–29.

54. *FEER,* January 1, 1987, pp. 10–13.

55. Ibid., p. 11.

56. *FEER,* December 25, 1986, pp. 14–15.

57. AFP, September 22, 1986, FBIS *Daily Report, East Asia,* September 23, 1986.

58. *FEER,* December 25, 1986, pp. 14–16.

59. The English-language *China Daily* argued China was acting in self-defense along the border. See January 8, 1986, p. 1.

60. An article in the *Washington Post* indicates that this was the reason for the fighting. See January 8, 1986, p. A30.

61. Chang, "Beijing Versus Hanoi," p. 598.

Chapter 4

1. *Los Angeles Times,* March 13, 1987.

2. *FEER,* February 5, 1987.

3. *FEER,* August 13, 1987.

4. *FEER,* August 27 and September 3, 1987.

5. *Renmin ribao,* September 4, 1987, FBIS *Daily Report, China,* September 4, 1987.

6. *FEER,* October 22, 1987.

7. Radio Beijing, FBIS *Daily Report, China,* November 17, 1987.

8. NCNA, October 13, 1987, FBIS *Daily Report, China,* October 15, 1987. See *FEER,* October 22, 1987, for Sihanouk's reaction.

9. *New York Times,* November 11, 1987.

10. *China Daily,* December 4, 1987.

11. *FEER,* December 17, 1987. See also NCNA, December 5, 1987, FBIS *Daily Report, China,* December 8, 1987.

12. *Christian Science Monitor,* December 9, 1987. China's reportage of the talks covered more of the Chinese viewpoint of the Cambodian conflict, predictably noting the necessary precondition of a Vietnamese withdrawal before meaningful talks could occur. See *China Daily,* December 7, 1987.

13. *Christian Science Monitor,* January 12, 1988.

14. *Renmin ribao,* December 11, 1987, FBIS *Daily Report, China,* December 11, 1987.

15. Radio Beijing, December 11, 1987, FBIS *Daily Report, China,* December 11, 1987.

16. *China Daily,* January 9 and January 14, 1988.

17. *Christian Science Monitor,* January 20, 1988.

18. Kyodo, January 21, 1988, FBIS *Daily Report, East Asia,* January 21, 1988.

19. *New York Times,* January 21, 1988.

20. *Renmin ribao,* January 21, 1988, FBIS *Daily Report, China,* January 23, 1988.

21. AFP, January 28, 1988, FBIS *Daily Report, East Asia,* January 28, 1988.

22. *Christian Science Monitor,* February 2, 1988.

23. *China Daily*, February 2, 1988.

24. AFP, February 3, 1988, FBIS *Daily Report, East Asia*, February 3, 1988.

25. *China Daily*, February 5, 1988.

26. Radio Beijing, February 11, 1988, FBIS *Daily Report, China*, February 11, 1988.

27. *FEER*, February 11, 1988.

28. AFP, February 17, 1988, FBIS *Daily Report, East Asia*, February 17, 1988.

29. *FEER*, March 3, 1988.

30. Ibid.

31. AFP, March 29, 1988, FBIS *Daily Report, East Asia*, March 30, 1988.

32. *Christian Science Monitor*, May 17, 1988.

33. *China Daily*, May 20, 1988.

34. AFP, FBIS *Daily Report, East Asia*, May 26, 1988.

35. *China Daily*, June 10, 1988.

36. Kyodo, June 13, 1988, FBIS *Daily Report, East Asia*, June 13, 1988.

37. Hanoi Domestic Service, June 16, 1988, FBIS *Daily Report, East Asia*, June 17, 1988.

38. *China Daily*, June 17, 1988.

39. *FEER*, June 23, 1988.

40. *Washington Post*, June 18, 1988.

41. *China Daily*, June 27, 1988.

42. *FEER*, June 30, 1988.

43. *Washington Post*, July 15, 16, 1988.

44. *New York Times*, January 22, 1988.

45. *Washington Post*, July 15, 22, 1988.

46. *Washington Post*, July 1, 2, 1988.

47. NCNA, July 1, 1988, FBIS *Daily Report, China*, July 1, 1988.

48. *Washington Post*, July 4, 1988.

49. *China Daily*, July 2, 1988.

50. VNA, July 7, 1988, FBIS *Daily Report, East Asia*, July 8, 1988.

51. *Washington Post*, July 8, 30, and August 2, 1988.

52. *Washington Post*, July 9, 1988.

53. *Renmin ribao*, July 12, 1988, FBIS *Daily Report, China*, July 14, 1988.

54. AFP, July 14, 1988, FBIS *Daily Report, East Asia*, July 14, 1988.

55. See *Washington Post*, July 26, 1988, for a review of the first day's events of the JIM.

56. *New York Times*, July 28, 1988.

57. *FEER*, August 25, 1988, p. 25. Sihanouk told Margaret Thatcher he thought the Khmer Rouge were worse than the Vietnamese.

58. AFP, August 16, 1988, FBIS *Daily Report, China*, August 16, 1988.

59. Ibid.

60. *FEER*, September 1, 1988, p. 32.

61. Beijing International Service, August 28, 1988, FBIS *Daily Report, China*, August 30, 1988.

62. NCNA, September 14, 1988, FBIS *Daily Report, China,* September 15, 1988.

63. *FEER,* September 22, 1988, p. 23

64. Kyodo, August 17, 1988, FBIS *Daily Report, East Asia,* August 17, 1988.

65. VNA, September 29, 1988, FBIS *Daily Report, East Asia,* September 30, 1988.

66. *FEER,* November 3, 1988, p. 17.

67. Prime Minister Hun Sen also stated that a political role for the KR must not include Pol Pot, Ieng Sary, Ient Thirit, Khieu Samphan, Son Sen, Ta Mok, Noun Chea, and Ker Pok. See AFP, October 28, 1988, FBIS *Daily Report, East Asia,* October 28, 1988.

68. *FEER,* December 1, 1988, p. 34.

69. NCNA, November 30, 1988, FBIS Daily Report, China, December 1, 1988.

70. *FEER,* December 15, 1988, pp. 16–17.

71. NCNA, December 13, 1988, FBIS *Daily Report, China,* December 15, 1988.

72. AFP, January 11, 1989, FBIS *Daily Report, China,* January 11, 1989.

73. *Wen Wei Pao,* January 22, 1989, FBIS *Daily Report, China,* January 23, 1989.

74. Sihanouk mentioned that the anti-Vietnamese resistance forces would fight with arms they had stockpiled, even if Beijing cut their support. See Kyodo, February 7, 1989, FBIS *Daily Report, China,* February 8, 1989.

75. Zhongguo Xinwen, February 1, 1989, FBIS *Daily Report, China,* February 1, 1989.

76. AFP, February 10, 1989, FBIS *Daily Report, China,* February 10, 1989.

77. *New York Times,* February 23, 1989.

78. AFP, March 14, 1989, FBIS *Daily Report, China,* March 14, 1989.

79. *FEER,* May 11, 1989.

80. One month before the talks in Paris began, U.S. Secretary of State Baker announced Washington was willing to consider the possibility of a Sihnaouk–Hun Sen alliance and to drop all support for the Khmer Rouge. The Bush administration dropped the idea a few days later. See the *Washington Post,* July 6, 7, 1989.

81. *New York Times,* December 3, 1989.

82. *New York Times,* January 15, 1990.

83. *FEER,* June 14, 1990.

84. *Beijing Review,* July 9–15, 1990.

Chapter 5

1. Friedrich Kratochwil, Harpreet Mahajan, and Paul Rohrlich, *Peace And Disputed Sovereignty* (Lanham, MD: University Press of America, 1985), pp. 139–54.

2. Technical aspects of this section are borrowed from Office of the Geographer, Bureau of Intelligence and Research, U.S. Department of State, "International Boundary Study No. 38, China-Vietnam Boundary, December 15, 1978."

3. Ibid., p. 1.

4. Ibid., pp. 2–3.

5. Ibid., p. 3.

6. See the text of the treaty in "Convention complementary to the convention for the delimitation of the frontier between Tonkin and China, of June 26, 1887, June 20, 1895." Reprinted in "Number 1895/4," of *Treatises and Agreements With and Concerning China, 1894–1919*, ed. John V.A. MacMurray (New York: Oxford University Press, 1921), pp. 26–35. As a matter of illustration to point out the ambiguity of the delineation of the boundary line, the text in Articles I and II of the treaty reads: "The frontier line leaves point r, runs north-eastward to Man-mei, then from Man-mei in a west-and-east direction to Nan-na on the Ts'ing-chouei-ho. . . . From point A it follows . . . the watershed."

7. "International Boundary Study," p. 7.

8. Foreign Ministry, "Memorandum on Chinese Provocations and Territorial Encroachments." Reported by VNA, FBIS *Daily Report, East Asia,* March 19, 1979.

9. Han Nianlong, "The Truth About the Sino-Vietnamese Boundary Question," a speech delivered at the fourth plenary meeting of the Sino-Vietnamese negotiations at the vice foreign minister level on May 12, 1979. Reprinted in *Beijing Review,* May 25, 1979, pp. 14–19.

10. "International Boundary Study," pp. 1, 9.

11. Foreign Ministry memo, March 16, 1979, FBIS *Daily Report, China,* March 19, 1979.

12. Han, "Sino-Vietnamese Boundary Question."

13. See the foreign ministry statements from both the PRC and SRV mentioned above, plus *FEER,* March 16, 1979, and *South China Morning Post,* March 28, 1977.

14. Xin Hua Commentator, "How Did the Sino-Vietnamese Border Dispute Come About," *Beijing Review,* May 25, 1979.

15. SRV foreign ministry statement, May 16, 1979. DRV Indochina Files.

16. *Beijing Review,* May 25, 1979.

17. See the proposals outlined in the two countries' memos mentioned above, and UN documents of the General Assembly, AS/doc31 and AC/921.

18. Armed conflict along the Sino-Vietnamese border increases during Vietnam's dry-season offensives against the Khmer Rouge in Cambodia, as the PRC attempts to drain Vietnam economically and militarily by promoting conflict on two fronts.

19. See chapter four for a discussion of this point.

20. For a more complete description of the physical characteristics of the Paracels and Spratlys, see Marwyn S. Samuels, *Contest for the South China Sea* (New York: Methuen, 1982), pp. 183–94. See also Dieter Heinzig, *Dis-*

puted Islands In The South China Sea (Wiesbaden: Otto Harrassowitz, 1976), pp. 14–19.

21. "Explanatory of the Provisions of the Commercial Convention between France and China of June 20, 1895, and of the Railway Contract of June 5, 1896. The Tsungli Yamen to Mr. Gerard, Minister of the French Republic at Peking." Note 1, Section 6, in *Treatises and Agreements Concerning China,* ed. MacMurray, p. 34.

22. See Part II, Article 3 of the UN Convention on the Law of the Sea. The text reads: "Every state has the right to establish the breadth of its territorial sea up to a limit not exceeding 12 nautical miles." Part V, Article 57 of the convention holds that the exclusive economic zone "shall not extend beyond 200 nautical miles from the baselines from which the breadth of the territorial sea is measured." Though both the SRV and PRC agree to the legality of this document, the difference lies in where the baseline actually lies. As long as this disagreement persists, reference to the UN Law of the Sea can have little bearing on the dispute surrounding the Gulf of Tonkin and the islands. See *The Third United Nations Conference on the Law of the Sea* (New York: Oceana, 1983), A/conf.62/122; October 7, 1982.

23. *FEER,* August 7, 1981, pp. 28–30. Also see "International Boundary Study," pp. 5–9.

24. *Beijing Review,* May 25, 1979, and FBIS *Daily Report, East Asia,* March 19, 1979.

25. *Third United Nations Conference on the Law of the Sea,* Annex VIII and Annex IX, pp. B208-B217.

26. I will use the Western names of the island archipelagos in order to avoid the biases associated with the Vietnamese and Chinese names.

27. People's Republic of China, Ministry of Foreign Affairs, "China's Indisputable Sovereignty Over the Xisha and Nansha Islands," *Beijing Review,* February 18, 1980, p. 21.

28. SRV, Ministry of Foreign Affairs, *White Book: The Hoang Sa and Truong Sa Archipelagos—Vietnamese Territories,* January 18, 1982, FBIS *Daily Report, East Asia,* January 18, 1982.

29. "Statement of the Chinese Ministry of Foreign Affairs," *Beijing Review,* January 25, 1974, pp. 3–4.

30. *Washington Post,* April 20, 1975, p. 14.

31. Ministry of Foreign Affairs, *White Book: Hoang Sa and Truong Sa,* p. 16.

32. *FEER,* August 7, 1981, p. 28.

33. SRV Foreign Ministry memo, FBIS *Daily Report, East Asia,* March 19, 1978.

34. Ibid., p. 28; also "Xisha and Nansha Islands Belong to China," *Beijing Review,* May 25, 1979.

35. *Beijing Review,* February 18, 1980, pp. 15–24.

36. "The Hoang Sa and Truong Sa Archipelagos," *Vietnam Courier,* January 4, 1982, in FBIS *Daily Report, East Asia,* January 4, 6, 8, 12, 13, 1982.

37. Ibid., January 12, 1982.

38. Republic of Vietnam, Ministry of Foreign Affairs, *White Book on the Hoang Sa and Truong Sa Islands* (Saigon: 1975). The arguments forwarded by Hanoi's white book of 1982 are almost identical to those posited in this document. China has used this as evidence against Hanoi in stating Beijing's position that Hanoi used to back China's claim to the islands before Vietnam was reunited.

39. More than 25 percent of the world's crude oil passes through the South China Sea. See *FEER*, August 7, 1981, p. 26.

40. *Christian Science Monitor*, November 5, 1986, p. 10.

41. Though the presence here is not thought to be great. Most of the military personnel on the islands are marines, placed there to guard the islands and watch area waters. Most of the naval crafts are small boats that can be used to harass the Vietnamese and watch the Soviet Union, but cannot carry on any prolonged war effort.

42. *FEER*, March 16, 1979, pp. 10–12.

43. *China Daily*, March 15, 1988; and *Christian Science Monitor*, March 16, 1988.

44. *New York Times*, March 18, 1988; and AFP, March 27, 1988, FBIS *Daily Report, East Asia*, March 28, 1988.

45. VNA, April 26, 1988, FBIS *Daily Report, East Asia*, April 28, 1988.

46. *FEER*, May 5, 1988.

47. *China Daily*, May 25 and June 3, 1988.

48. *China Daily*, June 10, 1988.

49. Current figures are difficult to obtain, but total imports of oil from the Soviet Union in 1982 were estimated to be 1.5 million tons, or all of that used by the SRV. See *FEER*, January 6, 1983, pp. 79–80.

50. Estimates from *Offshore* (May 1986): 118.

51. During the early months of 1984, it was apparent that things were not going well for the Vietnamese-Soviet drillers. Many of the wells drilled were either dry or low producers until the strike in April 1986, which was described as a "gusher." See *FEER*, May 24, 1986, p. 82, and *Oil and Gas Journal*, February 3, 1986, p. 28.

52. *Oil and Gas Journal*, February 3, 1986, p. 110.

53. Estimates for oil production are taken from Mark J. Valencia, *South-East Asian Sea: Oil Under Troubled Waters* (Oxford: Oxford University Press, 1985), p. 20.

54. NCNA, November 16, 1987, FBIS *Daily Report, China*, November 18, 1987.

55. The warnings coming out of China and Vietnam in regard to oil exploration in disputed territories are frequent. See *FEER*, August 7, 1981.

56. *FEER*, September 28, 1979, p. 19.

57. *China Business Review* 12, 1 (January-February 1985): 8.

58. Japanese companies are already involved with Chinese oil interests and could be moving towards agreements with Hanoi as well. In addition, India, Italy, Belgium, and others have expressed an interest in the Vietnam-

ese deposits. See *Petroleum Economist* (July 1985): 269 and *Oil and Gas Journal*, February 3, 1986, p. 28.

59. *Bangkok Post*, May 24, 1988, FBIS *Daily Report, East Asia*, May 25, 1988.

Chapter 6

1. Bureau of the Census, U.S. Department of Commerce, *The Population of Vietnam*, International Population Report no. 77 (Washington, DC: 1986), p. 9.

2. Victor Purcell, *The Chinese in Southeast Asia* (London: Cambridge University Press, 1952), p. 210.

3. Pao-min Chang, *Beijing, Hanoi, and the Overseas Chinese* (Berkeley: University of California Press, 1982), pp. 20–23.

4. Marilou Fromme et al., *Minority Groups in the Republic of Vietnam* (Washington, DC: American University Press, 1966), p. 937.

5. Purcell, *The Chinese in Southeast Asia*, p. 233. The Hakka have lived in the area around Mong Cai since the fourteenth century.

6. Fromme et al., *Minority Groups in the Republic of Vietnam*, pp. 943–44.

7. Ibid., p. 998.

8. Purcell, *The Chinese in Southeast Asia*, pp. 238–40.

9. Ibid., pp. 240, 243–46.

10. Fromme et al., *Minority Groups in the Republic of Vietnam*, pp. 986–88.

11. Dennis Gosier et al., *Minority Groups in North Vietnam* (Washington, DC: Department of Army, 1972).

12. Chang, *Beijing, Hanoi*, pp. 1–17.

13. Lewis M. Stern, "The Overseas Chinese in the Socialist Republic of Vietnam, 1979–1982," *Asian Survey* 25 (May 1985): 524–25.

14. Alexander Woodside, "Nationalism and Poverty in the Breakdown of Sino-Vietnamese Relations," *Pacific Affairs* 52 (Fall 1979): 381–409.

15. Thien Tou That, "Vietnam's New Economic Policy," *Pacific Affairs* (Winter 1983–84): 691–712.

16. *Washington Post*, April 5, 1978.

17. *FEER*, May 5, 1978, pp. 10–11.

18. *FEER*, May 19, 1978, pp. 12–13, and May 26, 1978, p. 22.

19. *FEER*, May 12, 1978, pp. 9–10.

20. "Statement of Chinese Foreign Ministry on Expulsion of Chinese Residents by Viet Nam," *Beijing Review*, June 16, 1978, pp. 13–16.

21. *FEER*, June 16, 1978, pp. 10–12.

22. *FEER*, August 4, 1978, pp. 12–13, and September 1, 1978, pp. 8–9.

23. *Beijing Review*, June 2, 1978, p. 15.

24. AFP, August 17, 1979, FBIS *Daily Report, East Asia*, August 17, 1979.

25. *FEER*, June 16, 1978, pp. 10–12.

26. Ministry of Foreign Affairs, People's Republic of China, "Statement of Chinese Foreign Ministry on Expulsion of Chinese Residents by Vietnam," *Beijing Review*, June 16, 1978, pp. 12–17.

27. Hanoi Domestic Service, July 10, 1978, FBIS *Daily Report, East Asia*, July 13, 1978.

28. *Luat Hoc*, Hanoi, July 1978, pp. 7–16, FBIS *Daily Report, East Asia*, August 30, 1978.

29. Fromme et al., *Minority Groups in the Republic of Vietnam*, p. 949.

30. Ibid., p. 997.

31. *Tap Chi Cong San*, August 1978, pp. 21–26, FBIS *Daily Report, East Asia*, September 18, 1978.

32. Chung Hsi-tung, "China Seeks Settlement Through Consultation of Question of Chinese Nationals in Vietnam," a speech given at the First Session of China-Vietnam Talks on the Question of Chinese Nationals. Reprinted in *Beijing Review*, August 18, 1978, pp. 25–31.

33. Ibid., pp. 26–28.

34. "Those Who Leave: The Problem of Vietnamese Refugees," *Vietnam Courier*, July 18, 1979, FBIS *Daily Report, East Asia*, July 19, 1979.

35. *FEER*, June 15, 1979, pp. 10–12, and July 7, 1979, pp. 8–9.

36. Chang, *Beijing, Hanoi*, p. 60.

37. Ibid., pp. 59–60.

38. Stern, "The Overseas Chinese in the Socialist Republic of Vietnam," pp. 531–32.

39. Chang, *Beijing, Hanoi*, p. 35.

Bibliography

Government Documents

Finnish Inquiry Commission. *Kampuchea: Decade of Genocide.* Edited by Kimmo Kiljunen. London: Zed Books, 1984.

People's Republic of China. Ministry of Foreign Affairs. *China Seeks Settlement Through Consultation of Question of Chinese Nationals in Vietnam.* First Session of China-Vietnam Talks on the Question of Chinese Nationals. Reprinted in *Beijing Review,* August 18, 1978.

————. *China's Undisputed Sovereignty Over the Xisha and Nansha Islands.* Reprinted the *Beijing Review,* February 18, 1980.

————. *Chinese Government Statement, January 14, 1979.* Reprinted in *Beijing Review,* January 19, 1979.

————. *Comrade Hua Kuo-feng's Speech.* Reprinted in *Beijing Review,* November 23, 1977.

————. *Comrade Le Duan's Speech.* Reprinted in *Beijing Review,* November 23, 1977.

————. *Foreign Affairs Trends.* Secret PRC document translated by the U.S. Department of State. DRV Indochina Files. September 1979.

————. *Memorandum from Li Xiannian to Pham Van Dong, June 10, 1977.* Reprinted in *Beijing Review,* March 30, 1979.

————. *On Hanoi's White Book.* Reprinted in *Beijing Review,* November 23, 1979.

————. *Speech by Han Nianlong at Second Round of Sino-Vietnamese Talks in Hanoi.* April 26, 1979. Reprinted in *Beijing Review,* May 4, 1979.

————. *Statement on Expulsion of Chinese Residents by Vietnam.* June 9, 1978. Reprinted in *Beijing Review,* June 16, 1978.

————. *Supporting Kampuchea's Just Stand and Condemning Vietnamese Authorities' Aggression and Subversion.* December 5, 1978. Reprinted in *Beijing Review,* December 22, 1978.

————. *The Truth About the Sino-Vietnamese Boundary Question.* A Speech Delivered by Han Nianlong. Fourth Plenary Session of Sino-Vietnamese Negotiations, May 12, 1979. Reprinted in *Beijing Review,* May 25, 1979.

Republic of Vietnam. Ministry of Foreign Affairs. *White Paper on the Hoang Sa (Paracel) and Truong Sa (Spratly) Islands.* Saigon: 1975.

————. *New Document on Hoang Sa and Truong Sa.* Hanoi: April 26, 1988. FBIS *East Asia, Daily Report,* April 28, 1988.

Socialist Republic of Vietnam, Ministry of Foreign Affairs. *Report on the International Strategy of China.* June 1978. DRV Indochina Files. June 1980.

————. *Treaty of Friendship and Cooperation Between the Lao People's Republic and the Socialist Republic of Vietnam.* July 18, 1977. Reprinted in *Chinese Law and Government* 16, 1 (Spring 1983).

————. *Treaty of Peace, Friendship, and Cooperation Between the Socialist Republic of Vietnam and the People's Republic of Kampuchea.* February 18, 1979. Reprinted in *Chinese Law and Government* 16, 1 (Spring 1983).

————. *Treaty of Friendship and Cooperation Between the Socialist Republic of Vietnam and the Union of Soviet Socialist Republics.* November 3, 1978. Reprinted in *Chinese Law and Government* 16, 1 (Spring 1983).

————. *The Truth About Vietnam-China Relations Over the Last 30 Years.* Hanoi: October 1979. Reprinted in *Chinese Law and Government* 16, 1 (Spring 1983).

————. *White Book: The Hoang Sa and Truong Sa Archipelagos—Vietnamese Territories.* January 18, 1982. FBIS *East Asia, Daily Report,* January 18, 1982.

United Nations. 39th Session. *Communiqué for Investigation of War Crimes Committed by the Chinese Expansionists and Hegemonists Against the Socialist Republic of Vietnam.* A/39/153. February 23, 1984.

————. 35th Session. *Memorandum to the UN General Assembly on the Chinese Authorities' Frenzied Intensification of Their Criminal Schemes and Actions Against Vietnam since February 17, 1979.* A/35/105. February 1980.

————. 34th Session. *Opening Statements of the Vice Ministers of the People's Republic of China and the Socialist Republic of Vietnam.* June 28, 1979.

————. 34th Session. *Speech given by Phan Hien, Head of the Delegation of the Government of the Socialist Republic of Vietnam.* A/34/224 Annex. May 1979.

————. 34th Session. *Speech made by Han Nianlong, Head of the Chinese Government Delegation and Vice Minister for Foreign Affairs, at the Sino-Vietnamese Negotiations.* June 28, 1979.

————. *The Third Conference on the Law of the Sea.* A/conf.62/122. October 7, 1982. New York: Oceana, 1983.

U.S. Congress. Senate. Congressional Record. *Vietnam and China: An American Diplomatic Opportunity.* S 14348. August 24, 1978.

U.S. Department of Commerce. Bureau of the Census. *The Population of Vietnam.* International Population Report no. 77. 1986.

U.S. Department of State. *Agreement on Ending the War and Restoring Peace in Vietnam.* January 27, 1973. Reprinted in *Department of State Bulletin,* 68, (February 12, 1973).

————. *Da Nang Incident: June 1975.* DRV Indochina Files. June 1975.

————. *Indications of Strained Relations between China and Vietnam.* February 26, 1976. DRV Indochina Files. February 1976.

————. *Joint Statements by the Government of the United States and the Government of the People's Republic of China, February 21, 1972.* Reprinted in *Department of State Bulletin* 66 (March 20, 1972).

————. *Memo from Philip C. Habib to Secretary Henry Kissinger, September 13, 1975.* DRV Indochina Files. 1975.

————. *PRC's Emerging Policy in Southeast Asia.* DRV Indochina Files. December 1976.

————. *President Ford's Pacific Doctrine.* December 7, 1975. DRV Indochina File. 1975.

————. *SRV-PRC Relations: July 1976.* July 1976. DRV Indochina Files. July 1976.

————. *U.S. Repeats Veto of UN Admission of North and South Vietnam.* Reprinted in the *Department of State Bulletin* (October 20, 1975).

————. *USSR-SRV Economic Relations: November 1980.* Internal State Department Memo. DRV Indochina Files. November 1980.

————. Foreign Ministry of the People's Republic of China. *Joint Communiqué on the Establishment of Diplomatic Relations between the United States of America and the People's Republic of China, January 1, 1979.* Reprinted in the *Department of State Bulletin* 79 (January 1979).

————. Office of the Geographer. Bureau of Intelligence and Research. *International Boundary Study No. 38, China-Vietnam Boundary, December 15, 1978.*

U.S. White House. *Remarks of the President and Press* Conference of Leonard Woodcock, Chairman, President's Commission on MIAs. DRV Indochina Files. March 1977.

Press Reports

Agence France Presse
Associated Press
Baltimore Sun
Beijing Review
China Business Review
China Daily
Christian Science Monitor
Far Eastern Economic Review
Foreign Broadcast Information Service, *Daily Report, China Foreign Broadcast Information Service, Daily Report, East Asia*
Hanoi Domestic News Service
Hsin Wan Pao, (Hong Kong)
Kyodo News Service (Japan)
Los Angeles Times
Luat Hoc (Hanoi)

Philadelphia Inquirer
New China News Agency
New York Times
Quan Doe Nhan Dan (Hanoi)
Reuters
Renmin ribao (Beijing) [People's Daily]
South China Morning Post
Soviet News Agency TASS
Tap Chi Cong San (Hanoi)
United Press International
Vietnam Courier
Vietnam News Agency
Washington Inquirer
Washington Post

Archive Materials

National Chengchi University. Taipei. Institute for International Relations.
University of California. Berkeley. Institute of East Asian Studies. Indochina
    Archives. Democratic Republic of Vietnam Files.

Journal Articles

Chang, Pao-min. "Beijing Versus Hanoi," *Asian Survey* (May 1983).
Chauncey, Helen, and Lowell, Finley. "U.S. Policy and the Crisis in Asia,"
    Southeast Asia Chronicle 68 (1980).
Chen, King C., ed. *Chinese Law and Government* 16 (Spring 1983).
Hamrin, Carol Lee. "China Reassesses the Superpowers," *Pacific Affairs* 56
    (Summer 1983).
Jackson, Karl D. "Cambodia 1977: Gone to Pot," *Asian Survey* (January 1978).
Kelemen, Paul. "Soviet Strategy in Southeast Asia: The Vietnam Factor,"
    Asian Survey 24, 3 (March 1984).
Offshore (May 1986).
Oil and Gas Journal, February 3, 1986.
Petroleum Economist (July 1985), p. 265.
Robinson, Thomas W. "The Sino-Soviet Border Dispute: Background, Devel-
    opment, and the March 1969 Clashes," *American Political Science Review*
    66 (December 1972).
Stern, Lewis M. "The Overseas Chinese in the Socialist Republic of Vietnam,
    1979–1982," *Asian Survey* 25, 5 (May 1985).
Su, Se Chi. "China and the Soviet Union," *Current History* (September 1984).
That, Thien Tou. "Vietnam's New Economic Policy," *Pacific Affairs* 56 (Win-
    ter 1983–84).
Woodside, Alexander. "Nationalism and Poverty in the Breakdown of Sino-
    Vietnamese Relations," *Pacific Affairs* 52 (Fall 1979).

Books

Buttinger, Joseph. *A Dragon Defiant: A Short History of Vietnam.* New York: Praeger, 1972.

Buu, Lam Truong. "Intervention Versus Tribute in Sino-Vietnamese Relations, 1788–1790." In *The Chinese World Order,* edited by Fairbank.

Cairns, J.F. *The Eagle and the Lotus: Western Intervention in Vietnam, 1847–1971.* Melbourne: Lansdome Press, 1979.

Chang, Pao-min. *Beijing, Hanoi, and the Overseas Chinese.* Berkeley: University of California Press, 1982.

Chen, King C. *Vietnam and China, 1938–1954.* Princeton: Princeton University Press, 1969.

Craig, Albert M., John K. Fairbank, and Edwin O. Reischauer. *East Asia. Tradition and Transformation.* Boston: Houghton Mifflin, 1973.

Dommen, Arthur J. *Laos: Keystone of Indochina.* Boulder: Westview Press, 1985.

Duiker, William J. *China and Vietnam: The Roots of Conflict.* Indochina Research Monograph, no. 1. Berkeley: Institute of East Asian Studies, 1986.

Eisenhower, Dwight D. *Mandate For Change: 1953–56.* Garden City, New York: Doubleday, 1963.

Etcheson, Craig. *The Rise and Demise of Democratic Kampuchea.* Boulder: Westview Press, 1984.

Fairbank, John K., ed. *The Chinese World Order.* Cambridge: Harvard University Press, 1968.

Fromme, Marilou, et al. *Minority Groups in the Republic of Vietnam.* Washington, DC: American University Press, 1966.

Gosier, Dennis, et al. *Minority Groups in North Vietnam.* Washington, DC: Department of the Army, 1972.

Heinzig, Dieter. *Disputed Islands in the South China Sea.* Wiesbaden: Otto Harrassowitz, 1976.

Honey, P.J. *Genesis of a Tragedy: The Historical Background to the Vietnam War.* London: Ernest Benn, 1968.

Hsu, Immanuel C.Y. *The Rise of Modern China.* New York: Oxford University Press, 1986.

Karnow, Stanley. *Vietnam: A History.* New York: Penguin, 1984.

Kissinger, Henry A. *The White House Years.* Boston: Little, Brown, 1979.

————. Years of Upheaval. Boston: Little, Brown, 1982.

Kratochwil, Friedrich, Harpreet, Mahajan, and Paul Rohrlich. *Peace And Disputed Sovereignty.* Lanham, MD: University Press of America, 1985.

Lamb, Helen B. *Vietnam's Will to Live.* New York: Monthly Review Press, 1972.

Lawson, Eugene K. *The Sino-Vietnamese Conflict.* New York: Praeger, 1984.

Leonhard, Wolfgang. *Three Faces of Marxism: The Political Concepts of Soviet Ideology, Maoism, and Humanist Marxism.* New York: Paragon Books, 1979.

MacMurray, John V.A., ed. *Treaties and Agreements With and Concerning China, 1894–1919*. New York: Oxford University Press, 1921.

Mancall, Mark. "The Ch'ing Tribute System: An Interpretive Essay." In Fairbank, *The Chinese World Order*.

McAleavy, Henry. *Black Flags in Vietnam: The Story of a Chinese Intervention*. New York: Macmillan, 1968.

McLellan, David. *Marxism After Marx*. Boston: Houghton Mifflin, 1979.

Nixon, Richard M. *The Memoirs of Richard Nixon*. New York: Grosset and Dunlap, 1978.

Purcell, Victor. *The Chinese in Southeast Asia*. London: Cambridge University Press, 1952.

Sainteny, Jean. *Ho Chi Minh and His Vietnam: A Personal Memoir*. Chicago: Cowles Book, 1972.

Samuels, Marwyn S. *Contest for the South China Sea*. New York: Methuen, 1982.

Stuart-Fox, Martin, ed. *Contemporary Laos: Studies in Politics and Society of the Lao People's Democratic Republic*. New York: St. Martin's Press, 1982.

Tang, Troung Nhu. *A Vietcong Memoir*. New York: Harcourt Brace Jovanovich, 1985.

Taylor, Keith Weller. *The Birth of Vietnam*. Berkeley: University of California Press, 1983.

Valencia, Mark J. *South-East Asian Sea: Oil Under Troubled Waters*. Oxford: Oxford University Press, 1985.

Wich, Richard. *Sino-Soviet Crisis Politics: A Study of Political Change and Communication*. Cambridge: Council on East Asian Studies, 1980.

Woodside, Alexander Barton. *Vietnam and the Chinese Model*. Cambridge: Harvard University Press, 1971.

Speeches

Gorbachev, Mikhail S. "Speech given on Soviet role in the Asia-Pacific region in Vladivostok, July 28, 1986." See FBIS, *Daily Report, Soviet Union* July 29, 1988.

Index

About the Author

Steven J. Hood received his Ph.D from the University of California, Santa Barbara in 1987. He has taught at Brigham Young University and is currently assistant professor of politics at Ursinus College in Collegeville, Pennsylvania. He has published articles in *Asian Survey* and *Asian Thought and Society*. He is currently working on a book about China's Guomindang.

"Particulary valuable for contemporary use is the chapter on the Chinese-Vietnamese face off in Cambodia."

–Indochina Chronology

"The 1979 China-Vietnam War had important consequences for Southeast Asia but has received little attention in the West. Using a variety of official sources from the governments of the United States, China, Vietnam, Cambodia, and the UN, as well as a host of books and scholarly journals, Hood has put together an account that seeks, as he writes in the introduction, '[to] be easily understood by the informed nonspecialist, and yet enlighten the Asian scholar or specialist in conflict studies seeking greater understanding of this ongoing power struggle.' The book does exactly that, in a most effective manner. . . . An excellent selection for academic and larger public libraries."

—Library Journal

"A first rate, full scale examination of the 1979 Sino-Vietnamese War."

—Douglas Pike, University of California, Berkeley

An East Gate Book

M.E. Sharpe

Armonk, New York
London, England

Cover design by Ted Palmer

ISBN 1-56324-270-2

90000>

9 781563 242700